DRIVEN

December 3, 2017

DRIVEN

To John, this book on success - fr an international expert on "World Trade Center" and so many other world business ventures! Also on GloSal Peace

With my best regards,

CelebrityPress®
Winter Park, Florida

Chapter 4, pages 41 ++

CONTENTS

CHAPTER 1
MAXIMIZE YOUR INCOME
By Brian Tracy 11

CHAPTER 2
THE ALMOST-SUPERWOMAN
By Naheed Chowdhry 23

CHAPTER 3
WHO IS YOUR BEST EMPLOYEE? ...YOU!
By Roger Damon Moss 33

CHAPTER 4
A WINNING MINDSET – YOUR ROADMAP TO SUCCESS
—HOW STRATEGIC THINKING AND PLANNING WILL DRIVE YOU TO EXCELLENCE
By Jean-Jacques Vitrac 41

CHAPTER 5

PUT YOURSELF IN THE DRIVER'S SEAT: CREATING A PERSONA OF IMPACT

By Nick Nanton & JW Dicks 53

CHAPTER 6

TRAIN WRECK AT THREE MILES PER HOUR

By Max Hooper, PhD 69

CHAPTER 7

TEN SUCCESS PRINCIPLES

By Steve & Kelly McCarthy 81

CHAPTER 8

THE MOST COMMON MISTAKES ENTREPRENEURS MAKE WHEN STARTING AND RUNNING A BUSINESS

By Isaiah Colton 91

CHAPTER 9

WHY DID I STUMBLE PAST THE POINT OF NO RETURN?
—LEADING THE FUTURE OF HEALING

By John Parks Trowbridge M. D., FACAM 101

CHAPTER 10

MOVE UP TO CONDO PROFITABILITY

By Joseph Pazcoguin 119

CHAPTER 11

FROM ZERO TO THE TOP

By Georgi Gunchev 129

CHAPTER 12

RISE AND SHINE

By Darice Jordan 139

CHAPTER 13

ROCK BOTTOM TO E-COMMERCE ROCK STAR

—SEVEN STRATEGIES TO CREATING AND SUSTAINING SUCCESS

By Sam E. Cohen 149

CHAPTER 14

SIMPLE WAYS TO GUARANTEE YOU WILL NEVER RUN OUT OF MONEY

By Scott Zimmerman 159

CHAPTER 15

THE BROKEN MILLIONAIRE

—MY JOURNEY TO SPIRITUAL AND FINANCIAL WEALTH

By Demetrius Early 169

CHAPTER 16

THE ART OF LIVING

By Diane Thomas Galloway 179

CHAPTER 17
LIFE BEYOND THE SCAR
—THE POWER OF NEVER GIVING UP

By Danielle Gordon 189

CHAPTER 18
DRIVEN TO BE SUCCESSFUL IN BUSINESS

By Scott Burnett, Esq. 199

CHAPTER 1

MAXIMIZE YOUR INCOME

BY BRIAN TRACY

You have the ability, right now, to earn vastly more than you are earning today, probably two or three times as much, by changing some of the things you are doing each day. How do we know this? Simple. You are surrounded by people who are not as smart, as ambitious or as determined as you, who are already earning much more than you are. And all of these people started off earning less than you are earning today. In this chapter, I will show you how to move to the front of the income-line of life, and faster than you ever thought possible.

One of the qualities of top men and women is that they are extremely self-reliant. They accept complete responsibility for themselves and everything that happens to them. They look to themselves as the source of their successes and as the main cause of their problems and difficulties. High achievers say, "If it's to be, it's up to me."

When things aren't moving along as fast as they want, they ask themselves, "What is it in me that is causing this problem?" They refuse to make excuses or to blame other people. Instead, they look into themselves, and seek for ways to overcome their obstacles and to make progress.

SEE YOURSELF AS SELF-EMPLOYED

Totally self-responsible people look upon themselves as self-employed. They see themselves as the presidents of their own personal services corporations. They realize that, no matter who signs their paycheck, in the final analysis they work for themselves. Because they have this attitude of self-employment, they take a strategic approach to their work.

The essential element in strategic planning for a corporation or a business entity is the concept of "return on equity (ROE)." All business planning is aimed at organizing and reorganizing the resources of the business in such a way as to increase the financial returns to the business owners. It is to increase the quantity of output relative to the quantity of input. It is to focus on areas of high profitability and return and, simultaneously, to withdraw resources from areas of lower profitability and return. Companies that do this effectively in a rapidly changing environment are the ones that survive and prosper. Companies that fail to do this form of strategic analysis are those that fall behind and often disappear.

To achieve everything you are capable of achieving as a person, you also must become a skilled strategic planner with regard to your life and work. But instead of aiming to increase your return on equity, your goal is to increase your return on energy.

Most people in America, and worldwide, start off with little more than their ability to work. More than 80 percent of the millionaires in America started with nothing. Most successful people have been broke, or nearly broke, several times during their younger years. But the ones who eventually get to the top are those who do certain things in certain ways, and those actions set them apart from the masses.

Perhaps the most important thing they do, consciously or unconsciously, is to look at themselves strategically, thinking about how they can better use themselves in the marketplace; how they can best capitalize on their strengths and abilities to increase their financial returns to themselves and their families.

YOUR MOST VALUABLE ASSET

Your most valuable financial asset is your *earning ability*, your ability to earn money. All your knowledge, education, skills and experience contribute toward your earning ability, your ability to get results for which someone will pay good money. Properly applied to the marketplace, it's like a pump. By exploiting your earning ability, you can pump tens of thousands of extra dollars a year into your pocket.

And your earning ability is like farmland. If you don't take excellent care of it, if you don't fertilize it and cultivate it and water it on a regular basis, it soon loses its ability to produce the kind of harvest that you desire. Highly-paid men and women are those who are extremely aware of the importance and value of their earning ability, and they work every day to keep it growing and increasing with the demands of the marketplace.

One of your greatest responsibilities in life is to identify, develop and maintain an important marketable skill. It is to become very good at doing something for which there is a strong market demand.

WHAT ARE YOU GOOD AT?

In corporate strategy, we call this the development of a "competitive advantage." For a company, a competitive advantage is defined as an *area of excellence* in producing a product or service that gives the company a distinct edge over its competition. This "unique added value" enables the company to charge premium prices for its products and services.

To earn what you are truly worth, as the president of your

own personal services corporation, you also must have a clear competitive advantage. You also must have an area of excellence. You must do something, or several things, that makes you different from and better than your competitors.

Your ability to identify and develop this competitive advantage, this special skill, is the most important thing you do in the world of work. It's the key to maintaining your earning ability. It's the foundation of your financial success. Without it, you're simply a pawn in a rapidly-changing environment. But with a distinct competitive advantage, based on your strengths and abilities, you can write your own ticket. You can take charge of your own life. You can always get a job. And the more distinct your competitive advantage, the more money you can earn and the more places in which you can earn it.

THINK STRATEGICALLY ABOUT YOURSELF

There are four keys to the strategic marketing of yourself and your services. These are applicable to large companies such as General Motors, to candidates running for election and to individuals who want to earn the very most money in the very shortest period of time.

The first of these four keys is *specialization*. No one can be all things to all people. A "jack-of-all-trades" also is a "master of none." That career path usually leads to a dead end. Specialization is the key. Men and women who are successful have a series of general skills, but they also have one or two areas where they have developed the ability to perform in an outstanding manner.

THINK ABOUT THE FUTURE

Your decision about how, where, when and why you are going to specialize in a particular area of endeavor is perhaps the most important decision you will ever make in your career. As the strategic planner, Michael Kami, once said, "Those who do not think about the future cannot have one."

The major reason why so many people are seeing their jobs eliminated and finding themselves unemployed for long periods of time is because they didn't look down the road of life far enough and prepare themselves well enough for the time when their current jobs would expire. They suddenly found themselves out of gas on a lonely road, facing a long walk back to regular and well-paying employment. Don't let this happen to you.

In determining your area of specialization, put your current job aside for the moment, and take the time to look deeply into yourself. Analyze yourself from every point of view. Rise above yourself, and look at your lifetime of activities and accomplishments in determining what your area of specialization could be or should be.

KEEP YOUR MIND OPEN

You might be doing exactly the right job for you at this moment. You might already be specializing in an important area where people are eager to pay you a lot of money for what you do. Your current work might be ideally suited to your likes and dislikes, to your temperament and your personality. Nevertheless, you owe it to yourself to be continually expanding the scope of your vision and looking toward the future to see what skills you will need in the months and years ahead. Remember, as Peter Drucker said, "the best way to predict the future is to create it."

You already possess special talents and abilities that make you unique and different from anyone else who has ever lived. The odds of there being another person just like you are more than 50 billion to one. Your remarkable combination of education, experience, knowledge, problems, successes, difficulties and challenges, and your way of looking at and reacting to life, make you extraordinary.

YOU HAVE UNLIMITED POTENTIAL

You have within you potential competencies and attributes that can enable you to accomplish virtually anything you want in life. Even if you lived for another 100 years, it would not be enough time for you to realize your full potential. You will never be able to use more than a small part of your inborn abilities. Your main job is to decide which of your talents you're going to exploit and develop to their highest and best possible use right now.

What is your area of excellence? What are you especially good at right now? If things continue as they are, what are you likely to be good at in the future—say one or two or even five years from now? Is this a marketable skill with a growing demand, or is your field changing in such a way that you are going to have to change as well if you want to keep up with it? Looking into the future, what could be your area of excellence if you were to go to work on yourself and your abilities? What should be your area of excellence if you want to rise to the top of your field, make an excellent living and take complete control of your financial future?

KEEP YOUR EYES OPEN

When I was 22, selling office supplies from business to business, I answered an advertisement for a copywriter for an advertising agency. As it happened, I had failed high-school English and I really had no idea what a copywriter did. I remember the executive who interviewed me and how nice he was at pointing out that I wasn't at all qualified for the job.

But something happened to me in the course of the interview process. The more I thought about it, the more I thought how much I would like to write advertising. Having been turned down flat during my first interview, I decided to learn more about the field.

BACK TO SCHOOL

That day, I went to the city library and began to check out and read books on advertising and copywriting. Over the next six months, while I worked at my regular job, I spent many hours reading those books and taking notes. Each week, I applied for a copywriting job to a different advertising agency in the city. I started with the small agencies first. When they turned me down, I asked them *why*? What was wrong with my application? What did I need to learn more about? What books would they recommend? And to this day, I remember that virtually everyone I spoke with was helpful to me and gave me advice.

By the end of six months, I had read every book on advertising and copywriting in the library and applied to every agency in the city, working up from the smallest agency to the very largest in the country. And by the time I had reached that level, I was ready. I was offered jobs as a junior copywriter by both the number-one and number-two agencies in the country. I took the job with the number-one agency and was very successful in a short period of time.

THERE ARE NO LIMITS

The point of this story is that I learned that you can become almost anything you need to become, in order to accomplish almost anything you want to accomplish, if you simply decide what it is and then learn what you need to learn. This is such an obvious fact that most people miss it completely.

Some years later, I heard about a lot of people who had gone into real estate development and made a lot of money. I decided that I wanted to get into real-estate development and make a lot of money as well. I used my same strategy. I went to the library and began checking out and reading all the books on real-estate development that I could find. At the time, I had no money, no contacts and no knowledge of the industry. But I knew the great secret: I could learn what I needed to learn so that I could do what I wanted to do.

THE POSSIBILITIES ARE ENDLESS

Within six months, I had found an ideal piece of property for a shopping center on the edge of a fast-growing town. I then tied up the piece of property with a $150 deposit and a 30-day option. I immediately put together a proposal for a shopping center, as explained in the books that I had read.

With this proposal in hand, I tentatively approached several large potential anchor tenants, and several minor tenants, that together agreed to lease 85 percent of the square footage of this shipping center if I actually built it. Then I called on several large real estate development companies with my proposal and my tentative lease agreements. On the 30th day of my 30-day option, I sold 75 percent of the entire package to a major development company in exchange for the company putting up all the cash and providing me with the resources and people I needed to manage the construction of the $3,000,000 shopping center and the completion of the leasing. Virtually everything that I did I had learned from books written by real-estate experts, books on the shelves of the local library.

In the years since then, I have successfully bought, developed, built out, leased and sold more than $100 million worth of real estate.

THE SAME PRINCIPLES WORK

As you might have noticed, the fields of advertising and copywriting, and real-estate development, are very different. But these industries, and every business venture I have explored over the years, had one element in common. Success in each area was based on the decision, first, to specialize in that area and, second, to become extremely knowledgeable in that area so that I could do a good job and get results if I got a chance.

In looking at your current and past experiences for an area of specialization, one of the most important questions to ask yourself is, "What activities have been most responsible for my success in life to date?"

How did you get from where you were to where you are today? What talents and abilities seemed to come easily to you? What things do you do well that seem to be difficult for most other people? What things do you most enjoy doing? What things do you find most intrinsically motivating? What things make you happy when you are doing them?

INCREASE YOUR EARNING ABILITY

In becoming more valuable, in increasing your ability to get results that people will pay you for, your level of interest, excitement and enthusiasm about the particular job or activity is a key factor. You'll always do best and make the most money in a field that you really enjoy. It will be an area that you like to think about and talk about and read about and learn about. Successful people love what they do, and they can hardly wait to get to it each day. Doing their work makes them happy, and the happier they are, the more enthusiastically they do it, and the better they do it as well.

BECOME DIFFERENT AND BETTER

The second key to becoming more valuable is *differentiation*. You must decide what you're going to do to be both different and better than your competitors in the same field. Remember, you have to be good in only one specific area to move ahead of the pack. And you must decide what that area should be. What do you, or could you do, better than almost anyone else?

SEGMENT YOUR MARKET

The third strategic principle in making a lot of money sooner is *segmentation.* You have to look at the marketplace and determine where you can best apply yourself, with your unique talents and abilities, to give yourself the highest possible financial return on the amount of time and energy you invest. What customers, companies, products, services or markets, can best utilize your special talents and offer you the most in terms of financial rewards and future opportunities?

FOCUS AND CONCENTRATE

The final key to personal strategic planning is *concentration.* Once you have decided the area in which you are going to specialize, how you are going to differentiate yourself, and where in the marketplace you can best apply your strengths, your final job is to concentrate all of your energy on becoming excellent in that one area. The marketplace only pays extraordinary rewards for extraordinary performance.

In the final analysis, everything that you have accomplished up to now is a part of the preparation for becoming outstanding in your chosen field. When you become very good at doing something that people want, need and are willing to pay for, you will soon begin moving rapidly into the top ranks of the highest-paid people everywhere.

About Brian

Brian Tracy is one of the top business experts and trainers in the world. He has taught more than 5,000,000 sales people in 80 countries.

He is the President of Brian Tracy International, committed to teaching ambitious individuals how to rapidly increase their sales and personal incomes.

CHAPTER 2

THE ALMOST-SUPERWOMAN

BY NAHEED CHOWDHRY

Growing up in the port city of Karachi, Pakistan, my childhood was typical of the privileged little bubble encompassing most middle-upper class families. School was a home called St. Joseph's Convent, run by The Nuns, who ranged from darling (Sister Emily, so benign you could steal her chocolate from under her nose when she was looking the other way) to Sister Zinnia (as soon as you heard her footsteps, your heart sank, for you knew you could run but not hide from the punishment that was to follow). Those were the days of big hair, Madonna and moonwalking. Weekends were spent playing in the safe streets, cycling with friends and cousins, and playing night cricket under glinting fairy lights swinging gently in the wind, strung up across an empty plot of land from one house to the other.

Fast forward to when I began my corporate career with Unilever. Women in a corporate environment was the norm in urban centres. However, certain remarks were slipped in so subtly that you almost missed them. For example, Unilever was known as Lever Brothers back then; I remember my first manager used to snicker about how it was fast becoming "Lever Sisters."

It was a proud day when Unilever appointed their first female CEO in Pakistan, the incredibly dynamic Musharaf Hai. Not long after, my friend and I noticed the increase in the number of women who left soon after their first child was born, and successfully co-advocated setting up a day-care centre onsite.

I met Shahab at Unilever and we were married a few years later. Life spun me through Australia with Unilever, then back to Pakistan – where the first two of our four children arrived a few months earlier than expected. My determined family came together to ensure that every second of every day, our babies received more love than they could ever handle. Every morning, they would be strapped into their car seats and driven by me to my office, where they would be welcomed with open arms by the day-care staff; even the security guards would 'coo' over them. (In Pakistan, it is perfectly acceptable to 'coo' over any and every child.) In the evenings, they would head back home with me, where their doting grandmother and aunt would be waiting to help me feed them (and save them from their snappy, exhausted mom). Their dad exercised infinite patience with them and my mother-in-law would fly down from Lahore if either baby so much as sneezed.

The first two years flew by. Then suddenly, Shahab was posted to one of the Middle East hubs. I broke the news to my mother and in an ironic twist of fate, just before we were about to leave, she discovered the Lump that changed our lives. I think now that my mother knew she had little time left, even though the doctors assured her it could be eliminated through aggressive chemo. She put on a brave face right until the last day when we drove away to the airport.

Once again in a new region, I joined Mondelez. Shortly after, we learnt of baby no. 3. It was an unexpected ray of sunshine at a difficult time for all of us. My mother found the strength to fly in for a few days after her last chemo session to see her newest granddaughter, Ayla. Though she seemed strong, it would be the last trip she would ever make, for the cancer would return soon after she went back home.

That year was a blur. I returned to work after the designated six weeks of maternity leave. Thereafter, on every possible weekend, I would throw tiny, happy Ayla and my breast pump over my shoulder, hop on-board the red-eye to my mother, and return the following day. It would be a struggle to appear normal at work, in an environment where colleagues expected me to slip up with the pressure of a newborn. They knew little if anything about my mother; I deliberately kept it that way. In fact, an HR leader would later tell me I was considered cold and unfeeling as I did not cry publicly when I received the final news about my mother. I often wonder if the same reaction would have been expected of me had I not been a woman?

My mother passed away the following year, just after Ayla turned one. I was due to take the children for a farewell visit the next morning when I got the call. I was so mad at my mother for not having waited for me to say goodbye. That was my way of avoiding the guilt I felt at not being by her side during her final time.

Soon after, I left Mondelez for another role with a company called Groupe Bel Middle East. I made some of my dearest friends there and had some of the best times of my professional life. Here, I met another iconic leader, Marina Menu; she headed up the region, and always found time when in town, to share some invaluable mentoring advice. I marvelled at how expertly she navigated the power corridors with a mix of people- and result-orientation.

Unexpectedly, baby no. 4, Eleeza, decided to show up. Separate from our professional interactions, my supportive team and manager went to great lengths to ensure my comfort. To the extent that when we were travelling together, I'd always get the best room, the best seat, the best flights there and back. There was even a tiny empty corner office converted into a private space for me to express milk. My loyalty grew manifold and it showed in my work.

As a result, when Shahab was posted to Cairo, I was offered a promotion there with the Bel office. Unfortunately, it did not work out – it was the same year as the Arab Spring and too unsafe for me to move with four children aged 0 to 5.

With a heavy heart, I gave up work and took up a writing course. I penned my first Young Adults novel, *The Bubble Kids* – a tale set in Pakistan. This was one I wrote for the twins to help them understand how the values of friendship and love were universal and could triumph over any divide – be it cultural, ethnic or religious. My dream is for it to be read by children the world over. Perhaps one of them will use its principles to make a global difference.

Towards the end of that year, I was contacted for a role with The Hershey Company. I was excited by the sizeable role, looking after the EMEA (Europe, Middle East and Africa) region. I was also the only woman on the region's leadership team. However, the red flags started going off at my first appraisal, showing up again at my next one, when my manager kept insisting that I need to be the "mother" of the team (I was the only woman on the region's leadership team there). It was in sharp contrast to colleagues at the global HQ, who appreciated my work and provided constructive feedback in an objective manner. Further, I was fortunate to be one of a handful of women across the organisation that were individually mentored for some time by the current CEO, Michele Buck. I looked forward to those monthly calls, cherishing the opportunity to learn from her experience.

My role at Hershey expanded to cover an additional work project based out of Shanghai. Forced into an "influence without authority" mode, I had to quickly figure out how to engage such a diverse team. I learnt that if you just asked "how" to resolve a seemingly impossible situation (vs. "if" they could), the team would always come up with the solution themselves. Ensuring they were visible to senior leadership meant that members would move into an "ownership" mode and go the extra mile. I found that any mindset can be cracked and objectives beaten in this way. Later, I leveraged those people-engagement-learnings into another major project for Hershey in the UK, with similar success.

Yet no matter how outstanding my work, colleagues at my office would always find fault with me. The sexism, initially implicit, was now increasingly commonplace – I think the bewildered senior teams just did not want to, or know how to, handle this Pandora's box. My manager and local colleagues attributed the "issues" to my lack of team effort, yet they were unable to explain why business results were still being delivered on or ahead of target, and why my interactions with other teams were going so well.

Finally, I exited Hershey in 2015 following a "restructure" – after a review confirming I was on track for an HQ-based leadership role. The announcement was so sudden that some of the HQ-based colleagues I was reporting to, or working with, did not know about it until after it happened, and their shock was palpable. There were no other roles that were mutually agreeable, and I left the organisation wishing I had spoken up much, much earlier – instead of enduring the bullying and sexism.

2016 was a year of soul-searching and evolution for me. I had met with some incredible leaders around the world who I would never have reached out to had I remained in my previous roles. Today, I enjoy consulting for clients who are keen to build their businesses further using my multi-faceted experience. I have also met with countless women across continents who have stories like mine, and I am struck by how my experience is fairly commonplace. This has driven me to channel my learnings into the development of a global e-platform for women, called IWill, with encouraging interest and support from the UN Women Council and gender-parity experts.

Through IWill, I am determined to turn ivory tower speeches by well-meaning CEOs and COOs into real-time actions for women, to recognise and overcome gender-specific challenges at work. Further, sisterhoods are great, but at the end of the day, any plan to address parity must be holistic and include all genders.

Including and beyond the above, there are some life learnings that I would like to share:

1. **Challenges are gifts in disguise.** You can be a victim and everyone will sympathise and move on. Or you can ask how you can mould the challenge into an opportunity that you gift yourself, your friends, your children.
2. **Change is an enabler.** Sometimes change is forced upon us and at other times it is welcomed. Either way, it forces us into a *carpe diem* mode.
3. **Procrastination is the seducer of time.** The sooner you (calmly!) make it clear that certain behaviours (implicit or explicit) are not acceptable, the better it will be. If the immediate person is not willing to listen, go to the next. Someone will.
4. **Find the strong women.** In every organisation where I have grown, I have been mentored and guided by women at the top. They will help you through the bad times too.
5. **Knowledge is the only currency** that can overcome any form of aggression or divide – real or perceived. If you have experience or a skill that is unknown and beneficial to others, keep leveraging it – eventually, you will move the needle.
6. **Learn. From anyone and everyone.** What is it that the coffee barista can teach you about multi-tasking? What can you learn about positivity and hope from children? What can the humble CEO illustrate to you that the arrogant leader lacks?
7. **It's OK not to be a conventional Superwoman.** The real-life Superwoman is not a perfectionist, but comes up laughing with an idea for Plan B if Plan A fails. Forgive

yourself if Plan A doesn't work – it happens to the best of us.

8. **Gratitude lists.** No matter how low you feel, there is a ton of stuff you are taking for granted that someone else is praying for. My list of ten things every morning has never failed to make me feel better. It can be as simple as a daily cup of coffee, or to have eyes to appreciate a beautiful day, to have healthy children or parents.

9. **Look for the person beyond the immediate attitude or action.** Why is your colleague raising their voice or constantly lagging on timelines? Can you help?

10. **Finally: Be brave.** Bravery is not about being fearless; it is about being frightened and still moving forward.

About Naheed

Naheed Chowdhry is a global corporate executive, author, accredited coach and mother of four. Born and brought up in Pakistan, Naheed has worked and/or lived in Asia, Australia, the UK, China, Russia, North Africa and the Middle East. Naheed's experience spans extensive experience with bluechip FMCG/Consumer Packaged Goods companies, the Pharmaceutical industry and Management Consulting.

Naheed currently lives in Dubai where she runs a boutique management consultancy, Rainmaker Consulting. Her clientele includes businesses based in, or looking to enter, the MENA region. She leverages her span of experience across industries to reverse-engineer her clients' strategies and provide commercially viable growth accelerators. She is also a *Wall Street Journal* Opinion Leader and has been a keynote and host at various regional conferences of similar stature.

Naheed's other passion is the development of a gender-parity e-platform, IWill.global, that is set to launch in Q3 2017. Naheed has always been passionate about the welfare of women in the workplace, advocating and co-developing the first day care centre at Unilever in Pakistan, and one of the first globally. The insight for the project came from Naheed's own experiences as well as those of friends and colleagues around the world. IWill promises an inclusive approach to convert TedTalk inspiration into an actionable roadmap for the 'working woman next door.' IWill has gained interest and support from many gender-parity advocates around the world, as well as from the UN Women's Council.

As a result, Naheed is also a UN Working Group Member for Youth and Gender Equality and a UN Women Leadership Taskforce Member. An Adler-accredited coach, Naheed enjoys mentoring, and in the spirit of sharing her knowledge and experience, she has been appointed a Mentor for the Queen's Young Leaders' Programme – an initiative by the University of Cambridge to mentor selected young leaders from 60 countries.

On the family side, Naheed is mother to four young global nomads who keep her on her toes. They have taught Naheed to move from being a perfectionist to understanding that things will go wrong and solutions can and will be found. Naheed uses this insight to help shift mindsets from a victim to a doer approach; to approach every challenge with a "How-do-we-crack-this?" vs. a "Can-we-crack-this?" approach; and to help her clients and teams explore and adopt both conventional and unconventional ways of accelerating growth.

Naheed is a published author of a Young Adults novel, *The Bubble Kids*, an endeavour she undertook to illustrate to her children how values of friendship, hope and trust can span any divide. In her spare time, Naheed enjoys Improv, travelling, horse-riding and adrenalin-rush activities that push her to overcome fears.

You can connect with Naheed at:
- Naheed@iwill.global
- www.linkedin.com/naheedchowdhry
- via twitter @naheedc

CHAPTER 3

WHO IS YOUR BEST EMPLOYEE? ...YOU!

BY ROGER DAMON MOSS

Inspire your employees to excellence by your example.

There's a show that was on TV for a period of time called *Undercover Boss*. The show's premise was to have a business owner go undercover into their business and act as an employee—not the boss. And no one knew who they were, either! Many of these "bosses" suffered from the disillusion that their employees—people they'd never met—were happy and gave their best efforts to their job. Other bosses were simply curious about the dynamics of the employees they count on for so much, as well as the employees' opinions of the management and leadership of the organization. More often than not, the "bosses" walked away from those shows with some drastic, harsh realizations. Imagine believing you were "in charge" and "in control" only to find out...

- Your employees have a low morale, and they see it as your fault.
- The people running your business are going out of their way to do as little as possible.
- There is no employee loyalty to you or the business.

What can you do? You can't fire anyone, but something has to change. In real world situations, negative encounters such as the undercover bosses faced are not easy to handle. Even the owner of a company is human, after all. Add a bit of crushed ego to the fact that the business is probably facing other challenges such as poor sales and a struggling reputation, and you will be looking at a long uphill battle to change things around. Is it impossible to do? No, but it does take work…starting with one huge shift of mindset.

Drop the "boss" and strive to be "your best employee."

Lead by example. This is a lesson that's as old as time and has been proven to be a powerful way to get exceptional results.

LEADING BY EXAMPLE

Most—if not all—people don't build a business with the intent of having it ultimately fail.

I own many businesses, which include a trucking company, a real estate company, and some various franchises. I love being an entrepreneur, but I am the first to admit that I haven't always been smart about it. I've worked against my intuition and followed the crowd that cheered on the accolades about "being your own boss." Then things started to happen and I learned a valuable lesson.

The word "boss" is a toxic word that makes for toxic environments.

Sure, this is my opinion, but it's proven to be absolute truth in my businesses. People don't open up to and think of the boss as someone looking out for them, just over them. So, having the people that worked for my companies look at me and think I was only the boss did nothing to help grow my businesses. It set up a belief and expectation of what I was not, and what I was. Basically, it separated me from those I relied on to make my business run. That's when I knew that going with the flow had to go and I had to get back to my natural instincts about leadership.

I dropped the word "boss" and became the employee that set a good example—an example that I wanted my co-workers to emulate. Guess what I experienced? The people around me appreciated me more because I was on the ground level, never being afraid to do what they did and showing that all the positions and details of a business matter. If a truck was stuck in mud, I pitched in to get it out. If there was a backed-up toilet somewhere, I literally went into the trenches. This mattered—my title did not.

I know this is a business approach that doesn't work for a lot of people, whether they are the entrepreneur or the employee of an organization, but it works excellently for my co-workers and me. By being the owner of several businesses and being hands-on in all of them, I've tapped into the only way I can manage everything that needs to be done. I'm there participating, and when I can't be there, the example I set speaks about what needs to be completed in my absence.

WHO WOULD YOU RATHER BE?

When you pit in-your-face against on-the-line you'll get very different results.

Let's take a look at two different ways to show leadership in an organization:

The first type of leadership is the business owner that has worked hard to build their business and along with the title of "boss" comes big responsibilities. Starting with no one forgetting who you are all the way through to the way you choose to assess everything everyone else is doing. For this owner, employees are a means to production more than they are an asset and resource that is valued. And they only hire the best, only to realize that the best often burns out in the environment and moves on to a different job where they're more appreciated.

The second type of leadership a business owner can choose to demonstrate is one where they lead by example. They are not above anyone else and willing to do what it takes to take care of business. They give their best every day, and can be confident that when they are not on-site or in sight, that their co-workers can address everything. There's a sense of pride in the culture and everyone gets that they are in this together.

Which environment would you rather be in? The one where you are completely in control, but don't have really committed employees; or, the environment where you work cohesively and have each other's back? Whether you are financially invested in the business or not, you likely are choosing the leadership by the way of example. It feels better, and it sounds more fulfilling, as well.

Leading by example leads to excellence.

If you look at the best places to work today, both in larger corporations and in smaller organizations, you'll find that employee longevity is directly tied to their personal fulfillment from the environment they work in. It's not always the job, but the mindset of the leadership and management. Why not be a part of that type of energy? Regardless of the type of business, a friendly relationship with all employees makes for a greater experience.

BENEFITS OF BEING THE BEST EMPLOYEE

Through a different mindset, some of the best successes are experienced.

The best employee is the one who cares what's happening at their workplace and with their co-workers. They don't just look out for themselves; they are alert to what their co-workers are experiencing, too. As I'd mentioned, the style of leadership I'm sharing isn't for everyone, and that's okay. So much good has come out of me doing this, though, and following my instincts about the right way to work, that I've experienced really exciting results from what comes naturally to me. The benefits are worth the approach.

It's important for you to understand some insight about what being the best employee is NOT:

❖ It is not being soft or a pushover. You can be an employee and still take your financial responsibilities seriously as an entrepreneur and business owner.

❖ It is not being a micromanager. It's only ego and a fear of not having the right systems in place that lead most people to micromanage. When your co-workers lead by example, they will cover things when you are not there, and do it excellently.

The real inspiration lies in what a best employee is. Have you ever considered how beneficial it would be to flip that "old way of operating a business" on its ear and get results that not only lift up your profit margin, but also enrich employee lives? It is possible.

These are the outcomes that are possible from being the best employee:

1) You can thrive by ditching the "my-way-or-the-highway" mentality. When a business owner stops allowing new ideas and concepts into their business environment, they are eventually going to run into troubles. The perspectives and processes of the people who are doing the most work for you on the ground level are valuable, therefore a benefit to your business.

2) Through showing up for work and giving your best efforts you can relax when you take that hard-earned vacation.

Unless your business involves extensive travel, think of your vacation time like your employees think of theirs. Mark it out and don't abuse it.

3) The opportunity to have an inclusive relationship with employees. They will start thinking of you as a co-worker, not "hawk eyes" and then you become a valuable peer. And, yes, they'll know you have to make certain decisions, but they will trust that you're in the game for everyone, not just yourself. Furthermore, they will be more comfortable demonstrating to you through their actions why certain considerations may be worth considering.

4) You will be connected to all the nuances of your business that exist at all levels. You cannot undervalue the importance of experiencing all aspects of your business firsthand, as compared to hearsay from a chain of other managers. Your co-workers appreciate the initiative, as well.

From many years of conducting business as the best employee possible, the results of the efforts have really shown themselves to be in alignment with every entrepreneur's goal—to be successful in areas of business you enjoy. Less time is spent trying to recapture what is faltering and more time is spent focusing on the values that make for a good business: employee pride, customer service, and a good reputation.

A DIFFERENT CULTURE

Every entrepreneur has to assess their efforts periodically.
Next time you do that, consider what impact dropping the
title might have on your business.

Ultimately, when you cling to the mindset of being a boss, you become disconnected from your purpose. It's inevitable. However, when you strive to be the best employee you can be, you are that employee that others follow. Your lead means something because you're not just talking to people and telling them what to do, you're participating in the success at ground level. There is a great deal of value in that approach to leadership. No job should be considered too big for you.

Your success means so much more than the title
you could give yourself.

Take a few minutes to evaluate your current work culture. Is it going ideally and the way you want it to? Where do things fall short? It's a tough conversation to have with yourself, because your business is important to you. However, by having that conversation and giving an honest assessment of the condition of your enterprise, from ground level on up, you will learn that many of the answers to solve your biggest challenges lie in one place. And that is in you—the person who has the potential to become the best employee.

About Roger

Roger Damon Moss is the Founder and CEO of the Investment Firm, LINNEZ CORPORATION, formerly RM Highland Corporation.

He was raised in Buffalo, NY and studied Business at the University of Buffalo. Roger's passion for business led him to start his privately-held company in 2000, which invests in multiple entities.

Roger's hobbies include travel and golfing.

Contact information:
- info@linnezcorp.com

CHAPTER 4

A WINNING MINDSET – YOUR ROADMAP TO SUCCESS

HOW STRATEGIC THINKING AND PLANNING WILL DRIVE YOU TO EXCELLENCE

BY JEAN-JACQUES VITRAC

As a political adviser, business trainer or keynote speaker, you are often asked the same question: how to succeed in your own personal life and in your career... particularly if you are successful yourself. The question comes from college students as well as from senior corporate executives and politicians. Even highly successful men and women want to know how to maximize their achievements and climb to new levels of expertise and success. Money is not always their goal. Peer recognition and social status are often serious motivations as well.

Of course, the best scenario is to start asking yourself that question when you are in college or when you apply for your first job. But there is no particular age for planning a successful career. It is never too early or too late. The following are some strategic steps to a winning career. First, you need to think and plan strategically. Developing a strategy means allocating your (at times, limited) resources intelligently through a unique planning system, in order to outperform your competition in any field where you can succeed. This was my own strategy to success.

STEP ONE: <u>IT'S A CAREER, NOT A JOB</u>

As a student thinking about your future or as an experienced professional, never jump on the first available job, even if you really need to work. Instead, try to strategically plan for your entire career. What are you interested in? What are you good at? Who is your competition? Where do you see yourself ideally in the years to come? What is your real field of expertise? It is not necessarily what you chose as your college major. And by the way, if you have no college degree, it is not the end of the world either. Steve Jobs developed Apple without a college degree.

The most important move is to think strategically about your job as the first step of your career. It is not simply a job. It must fit into your overall expectations for your career, your life and your personal strategy for success. You must build up your professional image and personality to achieve the ultimate level of success you want to reach. Choosing your first job – or any type of job at any time in your life – should be a powerful statement to the world about who you are and who you want to be. *Think big, think long-term, and simply go for it!*

When I was contemplating my first job at the age of 23, I had two very distinct opportunities. On one side, I was offered a marketing position with Unilever in Paris. The interview went well and that multinational company with 400 brands was very attractive. The salary was also excellent, and I would have been working only five days a week. On the other side, I was offered a position as a journalist for the leading daily newspaper on the French Riviera, working six days a week for less pay than what I was offered at Unilever in Paris. I had to think strategically. Would I go for the salary alone, knowing that the cost of living in Paris was much higher than on the French Riviera? Or was I considering the global picture? Working for the press would bring me many attractive bonuses, particularly for a newlywed couple living on a relatively limited income. I would be invited, often with my wife, to prestigious events in Cannes or Monte Carlo. I would meet and interview many important people, including millionaires, corporate executives, politicians, movie stars, and renowned artists and painters. Most of all, I would learn about the world, political and business practices, and the important aspects of real life. I would also be able to freelance for other newspapers and magazines in Europe.

At that point, I also had to ask myself what direction I wanted to take my life. And if I was not quite sure yet, I knew that working as a journalist would expose me to many people and situations that would give me a priceless and unique experience. Since I was already interested in an international career and in being relatively free to move around the world, journalism was perfect on both accounts.

STEP 2: <u>BUILDING A GLOBAL NETWORK</u>

The richest people in the world look for and build networks,
everyone else looks for work.
~ Robert Kiyosaki

Living in Cannes, with access to the film festival and many other international events, I was soon in a key strategic position to better understand the global dimension of business and to meet with political leaders as well as with famous economists. One of them was Jacques Rueff, adviser to the French government, free market thinker and monetary system expert. As a journalist, I interviewed many of these people who answered my questions and formed my opinion at the same time, preparing me for the key political and financial positions I would acquire in the future.

I also joined clubs for the networking opportunities. Since I was interested in world issues, I joined the Junior Chamber of Commerce, an organization present in 110 countries and better known in America as the Junior Chamber International (JCI), with a membership of several hundred thousand young business executives worldwide. JCI wanted to expand in Europe and Africa and needed a development adviser. As an elected officer of that NGO[1] in France, I applied for this exceptional international staff position. Here again, *strategic thinking was the key to being appointed at that level.* With only two applicants at the final stage of the selection, we were both asked if we could attend the international convention in Mar-del-Plata in Argentina a couple of weeks later. I answered positively even though I was not sure I could resign from my job as a journalist or even pay for a trip to another continent. The other candidate was not so daring and I got the job.

This first international position was my opportunity to visit thirty-five countries on three continents every year for four years and to meet with United Nations officials and experts, heads of state, world politicians, key business organizations, and the media. It was also a chance to visit multiple companies and meet their executives, to address thousands of business leaders and entrepreneurs in hundreds of local clubs and Chambers of Commerce while developing an understanding for economy, diplomacy and international business. During these four years, I met with Queen Elizabeth of England, King Baudouin of Belgium, King Hassan II of Morocco, President Lech Walesa of Poland, President Richard Nixon, and countless other political and corporate leaders worldwide. I organized and chaired international conferences in Morocco, Tunisia and Ivory Coast, worked with United Nations agencies, American think tanks, and economic development institutions worldwide. This early phase of my career allowed me to build an international network for business and politics which proved to be essential to my future career. I was also able to work in the United States for two years and meet with key government officials who helped shape my political, financial and business vision of the world.

STEP 3: <u>DEVELOPING A COMPETITIVE EDGE</u>

Thinking strategically should lead you to act strategically, since planning should always precede action. At the age of 30, I was back in France to start a more traditional career in Paris with a leading postgraduate academic institution.[2] There, I joined the executive team while teaching international marketing to the management of major French and international corporations. Two years later, I published my first book about international trade[3] which was well-received by business and media alike. That gave me the competitive edge I needed to strategically plan and pursue my entire career in Europe and later in America.

I was soon hired by a leading European consulting firm in Paris as a political and business adviser, likely because of my book, public exposure through the media, and keynote speaking engagements. Bernard Krief, the company founder, had just written a book about marketing your career to succeed[4], and we were both very interested in personal and professional development through self-motivation. With Bernard Krief, I worked in French politics as an adviser to major elected officials, municipalities and regions. Bernard also gave me my first opportunity to work for Jacques Chirac, the future President of France, when Jacques wanted to be elected Mayor of Paris. I also worked for major corporations, such as Airbus Industries[5] in 1975, to audit the performance of the company and provide actionable strategies to its newly appointed CEO, General Jacques Mitterrand, brother of Francois Mitterrand, another future French President.

In 1975, this competitive edge which I strategically developed and promoted brought me to the Central Bank of France, for three years of research and strategic coaching on multinational corporations. The Central Bank wanted to better understand the financial strategies of these global corporations to better control them as a regulatory financial institution. At that time, I also met and worked with Jean-Claude Trichet, years before his nomination as European Central Banker in 2003.

During our lifetime, each of us is going to make multiple strategic decisions, consciously or not. *The more aware and the better prepared we are, the more efficient we will be, and the more successful our personal, corporate or political life will be.* In my case, in 1980 I reached a point where I wanted the privilege of freedom over the rigid infringement of European government on individual and corporate lives. It was time to move back to America for the second part of my career, and to raise our three children in the unique environment of California.

A MAJOR STRATEGIC DECISION

Shortly after the EU presidency of Jacques Delors (Brussels 1985-95), the European Union moved to become more of a federal State and to dictate major decisions to member nations. I had worked with Jacques Delors on a personal basis, meeting with him at his home in Paris before 1980 and later for a videoconference between California and Brussels. As early as 1979, I realized that the European Union could one day turn to more authoritarian posturing which was going to lead to Brexit in 2016, when Britain decided to leave the European Union through popular referendum. I also realized that the election of Francois Mitterrand in France (May 1981) could bring a decline of the French economy and increase the burden of government in all areas of life. I knew personally the Mitterrand family – his sister, Genevieve, and his brother, Jacques – and could predict what François would do if elected in 1981. *Thinking strategically is to use each bit of information available to you to plan your action and act strategically.*

I subsequently decided in the summer of 1980 to permanently move my family to California. I wanted to raise our three children in a "more freedom, less government" part of the world where the Silicon Valley and other high-tech corporations were engaged in a real search for excellence. For me, this was a major strategic shift which was thoroughly planned and turned out to benefit my family, business, career, and the community.

In 1983, under newly-elected Governor George Deukmejian, I became interested in developing business relations and trade missions between California and France. For twenty years, using my political network in Europe and in California, these missions were extremely successful, prompting me to start a private business incubator to help French companies develop export business to California, while California companies were engaging in various trade missions to France and Belgium.

Until then, business incubation was mostly provided through public institutions such as colleges and universities, helping create and grow young businesses by providing them with affordable space, necessary services, coaching, management training, and financial and technical assistance. I created a private environment to offer these services to startups in America, transferring European technology to the United States while bringing new business ventures and opportunities to California and Europe.

TEAM BUILDING FOR A HARVEST OF SUCCESS

After thinking and acting strategically comes the time to close the deal. I call that phase "the harvest of success." Independent entrepreneurs and consultants as well as major global corporate executives can experience this exhilarating phase. For an independent entrepreneur, adviser and business coach like myself who has been engaged in international operations between Europe and California since 1980, *it becomes very important to build successful teams capable of surviving startup difficulties and to drive them to a harvest of success.*

My second career in California required a winning mindset and a creative strategy since we were entering virgin and unchartered international territory. It also required a solid team spirit to create lasting ventures, inspiring a large number of individuals with domestic experience in the United States and Europe to "think globally, but act locally." Strategic thinking became more important than ever in this new international dimension and environment.

In 1989, for the bicentennial of the French Revolution, I organized an international videoconference via satellite between San Francisco, Paris, and the European Union in Brussels. This luncheon forum on global business was well attended by about 300 California entrepreneurs from the Contra Costa Council and the WorldTech Executives Network. Senator Barry Goldwater was the keynote speaker followed by several business speakers and myself on international trade.

The same year, the French government asked me to coauthor a book about doing business in California[6] which had quite an impact on European entrepreneurs. While writing that book, I realized that my mission in America was to bridge the gap between two continents, the old and the new, tradition and innovation, yesterday and tomorrow.

I developed industrial trade missions under Governor George Deukmejian (1983-1990) and the California Economic Development Agency. A similar program was carried over under Governor Pete Wilson (1991-1998) who kindly offered me a large hall at the California State Fair in 1992, in exchange for bringing an international exhibitor to Sacramento. I produced a multimillion dollar "Discover Provence" exhibit to encourage strategic ventures and international trade between the two regions.

These various international activities encouraged economic development and job creations throughout California and Europe. Several business ventures and successful startups can be directly credited to these personal initiatives. They have driven major success stories across two oceans and three continents. . .

NOTES:

1. NGO: non-governmental organization.
2. Institut Français de Gestion in Paris (French Institute for Business Management).
3. Découvrez l'Exportation (Ed. Chiron, Paris, 1974).
4. Faites le Marketing de votre Carrière et Réussissez ! (Ed. Dunod 1971).
5. Called Aérospatiale at the time, more recently known as EADS, with some 40,000 employees building Concorde supersonic passenger planes.
6. Californie - Collection Guide d'Affaires. Centre Français du Commerce Extérieur (CFCE, 1989).

About Jean-Jacques

Jean-Jacques Vitrac is an international business and political adviser, coach and worldwide keynote speaker. For over forty years, he has driven business executives and prominent politicians to success in their own career, and has also taught students and addressed thousands of entrepreneurs and business leaders in some thirty-five countries.

As executive director and international marketing professor at the Institute of Business Management in France (Institut Français de Gestion, Paris), Jean-Jacques wrote his first book on export strategies in 1974 (*Découvrez l'Exportation*, Ed. Chiron, Paris) when he joined Bernard Krief International Consultants as a business and political adviser.

Jean-Jacques conducted successful political campaigns for some renowned politicians, cities and counties in France, such as former French President Jacques Chirac and the French Riviera region (PACA). He also chaired a group of experts for the French Central Bank to study multinational corporations and their worldwide financial strategies. Global companies and institutions such as Airbus Industries, Institut Pasteur and Fiskars have been among his clients.

A California resident since 1980, Jean-Jacques has also conducted high-tech and biotech trade missions between the United States and France under Governors George Deukmejian and Pete Wilson. Major news media in Europe, Northern Africa, and the United States have covered his achievements in economic development and international trade, and he was featured on television programs in France and the United States. In 1989, Jean-Jacques coauthored *Doing Business in California*, a book published by the French government (CFCE) and organized a videoconference between California, Paris and Brussels to discuss high-tech and trade development. This global event, co-chaired by Senator Barry Goldwater and sponsored by Bank of California and AT&T, was organized in cooperation with the Contra Costa Council, the European Economic Council in Brussels and the World Technology Executive Network. Jean-Jacques also served on the board of the East Bay International Trade Council in Oakland (1996-97).

Between 1982 and 2000, Jean-Jacques Vitrac developed an international business incubator in California for European and Japanese startups, offering them access to the American and Pacific-Rim markets.

An associate of the World Trade and Development Group in Washington DC, Jean-Jacques is co-founder and International Vice President of the Global Strategic Research Institute in California. For over 20 years (1972-1992), Jean-Jacques has been a European board member of L'Entreprise de Demain (Forum for Tomorrow), a non-profit European think tank in Brussels working with King Baudouin of Belgium and the Club of Rome.

In 2015, Jean-Jacques Vitrac was elected as a French diplomatic adviser (Conseiller Consulaire de France) in the United States by the French-American community in ten of the western states. As such, he is an elector of the French Senate.

In 2013, Jean-Jacques Vitrac published a biography of Anne Beffort (1880-1966), the first woman in Luxembourg to earn a doctorate degree. In 2016, he published a Kindle book in French on American presidential elections.

To contact Jean-Jacques:
- www.worldtradepartnership.com/p1891.html
- www.AnneBeffort.com

CHAPTER 5

PUT YOURSELF IN THE DRIVER'S SEAT: CREATING A PERSONA OF IMPACT

BY NICK NANTON & JW DICKS

Al Gore was supposed to be a sure thing.

In January of 2000, Gore was coming off serving as the Vice President in the popular two-term presidency of Bill Clinton, who still enjoyed over a 60% approval rating despite the Monica Lewinsky scandal. The economy was in great shape and there was no reason to see trouble for Gore, who was running to replace his boss.

Except some Democrats still did…

Throughout his career, Gore's public appearances were tagged with words like "wooden," "pedantic" and "boring." Clinton's charm and charisma, of course, completely overshadowed Gore during their 1992 and 1996 runs, but Gore, in turn, was important for adding some stolid stability to the freewheeling Clinton campaign.

But stolid stability wasn't the most wonderful asset when it came to running for President in the age of the media masters like Clinton. Voters wanted someone who could make them feel good and command their attention—and Gore would be hard-pressed to deliver that kind of excitement in the run-up to November.

That's why, exactly one year earlier in November of 1999 as Gore was gearing up for his run, feminist Naomi Wolf was hired to help transform him into an "alpha male." She advised him on wardrobe and attitude and charged the campaign $15k a month for her services. The problem was, *Time* magazine found out and printed the story, which made Gore look ridiculous from the outset.

And then came the debates.

In the first debate, most observers thought Gore came across as more knowledgeable and nuanced than Bush. However, most observers also thought Gore acted really, really weird. When Bush answered a question, Gore would contort his face and sigh loudly or roll his eyes, like he was in a silent film comedy. The sketch show *Saturday Night Live* viciously made fun of his tactics. In the second debate, Gore seemed to learn his lesson and stop over-acting. Unfortunately, he just appeared as the wooden bore his handlers were afraid he would be.

Then came the third debate and the strangest Al Gore moment of the campaign. After Bush answered a question, Gore walked away from his podium and towards Bush, stopping a few feet away from him and glaring at him silently.

Bush merely turned towards the Vice President, gave him a preemptive nod, and turned back to the audience.

Even though many thought Gore's command of the issues was far greater than Bush's, people were left feeling uncomfortable about the VP. One woman summed it all up by saying, "He had a different persona in every debate." All of which resulted in a close election nobody thought would be close, and George W. Bush becoming the next President of the United States instead of Al Gore.

In this age, every successful politician has to be what we call a "MediaMaster," someone whose *personal persona* must connect with the voters in order to triumph at the ballot box. And the same goes for most successful entrepreneurs.

In this excerpt from our forthcoming book, *Impact*, you're going to learn what we believe is the biggest secret to conquering your niche and drawing the most loyal, fervent following possible: Crafting a **Persona of Impact**.

What is a Persona of Impact? It's a personality-based style of communication that goes beyond the universal basics, built specifically on *who you are* and your *distinct personal qualities.* It's great to become as polished and professional as possible in your media presentations. However, if you don't also create your own *individual* appeal, your audience will have difficulty truly bonding with you as a person – especially if, like Al Gore did in 2000, you keep changing that persona willy-nilly. That, in turn, will limit your overall influence as a MediaMaster, causing you to be acceptable – but forgettable.

No matter what you think of Donald Trump, remember that, as he faced the first 2016 state primaries, he was running against 16 other Republican candidates. It was one of the biggest fields ever put forward by the party, but Trump easily dominated from the start simply because he was *not like anyone else.* More importantly, he was very comfortable *being himself.*

While everyone else tried to toe the traditional candidate line, mouthing the standard political platitudes, Trump didn't tamp down his usual brash way of talking. Instead he doubled down on it. Expected frontrunners fell by the wayside, because they seemed colorless and ineffectual next to Trump. You may argue over who was the most qualified candidate – but you can't argue over who was the most memorable candidate. His success was the ultimate triumph of the MediaMaster.

So how do you craft your own Persona of Impact? How do you tap into the special qualities that make you unique – and then leverage them to increase your MediaMaster magnetism?

Let's explore…

CELEBRITY BRANDING® YOU

Celebrity Branding® You was the title of our first Best-Selling book. Its ideas helped lay the groundwork for our Celebrity Branding® Agency by articulating the importance of establishing a personality-driven personal brand. We've been able to successfully help our clients do just that over the years; in the process, we've continued to learn more and more secrets about making that personal brand as powerful as possible.

It all begins with really understanding what a brand is all about. As defined in Wikipedia, a brand is *"a set of marketing and communication methods that help to distinguish a company from competitors and create a lasting impression in the minds of customers."* In other words – a brand is a way to differentiate one product from another, all things being equal.

And when all things became equal is when companies originated the whole concept of brands in the first place. By the 1950s, manufacturing technology had evolved to a point where most companies were offering products of similar quality. That was when the necessity of creating a "brand" became apparent, because those companies needed a way to set themselves apart from the competition. Here's how the evolution was described in an article from *The Atlantic*, "How Brands Were Born: A Brief History of Modern Marketing":

A brand manager would be responsible for giving a product

an identity that distinguished it from nearly indistinguishable competitors. This required an understanding of the target consumer and what we call a "branded proposition" that offered not only functional but also emotional value. Over time, the emotional value would create a buffer against functional parity. As long as the brand was perceived to offer superior value to its competitors, the company offering the brand could charge a little more for its products.[1]

Swap out "product" with "professional," "entrepreneur," "business owner" or "CEO" and the above paragraph still holds true.

Let's say you're a personal injury lawyer – obviously, there's a ton of others in that very same field. Why should people choose you over the rest? Easy answer – if you've established yourself as THE personal injury lawyer in your area. When the public sees your name on a daily basis in commercials, when they see you regularly pop up in online and offline media as a recognized personal injury expert, when they come into your lobby and see a rack of books that you've written on the law, they immediately associate you with being a top-tier professional. That results in them ascribing much more value to retaining you, rather than some other attorney. You've created a prestigious (and lucrative) personal brand – a brand that is based on *what persona you project in the marketplace.*

That projection *must* be purposeful. In other words, you must have a set of goals in place and methods of achieving those goals when it comes to cementing your Persona of Impact in the public mind.

A Relatable Persona

As you're building your Persona of Impact, you should understand that the way we think about brands in the 21st Century has radically changed.

1. Marc de Swaan Arons, "How Brands Were Born: A Brief History of Modern Marketing," The Atlantic, October 3, 2011

In the past, brands were an object or a hard-and-fast idea to be experienced from afar. You didn't think about having any kind of interaction with a Coke or a Pepsi, you just thought about buying the beverage and drinking it. But now, a brand is more about a *relationship*. As Sergio Zyman, author of *The End of Marketing as We Know It*, says: *"A brand is essentially a container for a customer's complete experience with the product or company."* [2]

There are several reasons for that. First of all, social media has empowered direct communication with companies and professionals, allowing easy access to a back-and-forth that never existed before. Second of all, innovative new companies like Uber, Lyft and Airbnb have created a whole new business model that's built more on a one-to-one experience. Starbucks also tends to operate as much as a community hub as a coffee shop and even airlines such as Jet Blue and Virgin America operate with more of a relationship vibe.

This trend is summed up by these remarks by Kira Wampler, CMO of Lyft: "Our original tagline was 'Your Friend with a Car' which served not only to describe the human, peer-to-peer experience we delivered with Lyft, but also to differentiate us from other private driver approaches." [3]

That's why it's more important than ever to craft your Persona of Impact as one that's both relatable to people and communication-friendly. The most successful personal brands are ones that reach and touch people on an emotional level, to the extent that the consumer believes they actually "know" that person. It takes some effort to pull off, but it's most definitely worth the effort – and the end result will be greater loyalty, engagement and differentiation.

---

2. Mark Bonchek & Cara France, "Build Your Brand as a Relationship," *Harvard Business Review*, May 9, 2016
3. Bonchek & France

The Optics of Oprah

Loyalty, engagement and differentiation. Those three attributes definitely apply to the personal brand of Oprah Winfrey, creator of one of the most powerful Personas of Impact in recent history and a top-tier MediaMaster who grew her success to the point where she now owns her own channel - a pretty substantial accomplishment for someone who grew up in poverty as a victim of abuse.

That success comes in part from her strong commitment to being herself. Oprah maintains an incredibly consistent persona – and she is aware of the amount of control she has over this persona. As she has said in the past, "I don't know what the future holds, but I know who holds it."[4]

It's a lot easier to maintain a consistent persona if that persona comes from a place of authenticity, something we recommend to all our clients. As Anna Wintour, the world-famous editor of Vogue, said of Oprah, "If you are out to build a brand, you have to know what is real and right for you. The choices that she has made stand the test of time because they are very personal choices."[5]

Your persona too, has to be a very personal choice. How could it be anything but? When you put on different personas like you're trying on a new jacket, you're setting yourself up to look as awkward and uncomfortable as Al Gore did when he walked over to George W. Bush on the debate stage and glared at him.

Instead, your persona has to be an integral part of your real personality. It has to tap into your best and most memorable qualities in the best and most memorable ways. Yes, you may have to work at projecting certain of your qualities and minimizing

4. John Baldoni, "Oprah Winfrey and Your Leadership Brand," *Harvard Business Review*, November 25, 2009
5. David Carr, "A Triumph of Avoiding the Traps," *The New York Times*, November 22, 2009

others that are irrelevant or don't add anything to the equation, but that's far different than, say, pretending to be a tough hombre from Waco, Texas when, in reality, you're a sensitive bookworm from Austin.

Just as important to the integrity of your persona is your actual *behavior*. People are used to "posers" – people who don't back up their words with actions. That's something you never caught Oprah doing – and something people shouldn't catch you doing, especially if you're asking them to trust you with their business.

HOW TO CREATE YOUR PERSONA OF IMPACT

So far, we've given a lot of general information about creating a Persona of Impact – but now let's get down to some nuts and bolts of how to actually make it happen. Generally, a Persona of Impact develops over time through a process of trial and error. But to help you jumpstart your development, we're going to share a five-step process created by leadership experts Norm Smallwood and Dave Ulrich[6] (and modified by us for the purposes of this chapter) that will help you build a strong, authentic, focused and engaging personal brand that will add incredible value to your persona.

Action Step #1: Work backwards from your goals

What do you want to achieve with your Persona of Impact in the next few years?

Do you want to become well-known? If you're already well-known, do you want to attract a certain kind of client or customer that you haven't been able to convert in the past? Do you just want to be seen as more of an influencer in your field? The answer will guide you in creating your Persona of Impact personal brand.

---

6. Norm Smallwood, "Define Your Personal Leadership Brand in Five Steps," *Harvard Business Review*, March 29, 2010

For example, if you are just looking for name recognition, you may want to do something clever to get your name in front of the public. Dr. Jonathan Zizmor was just one of hundreds of dermatologists in the New York City area when he began his practice. However, once he began putting his name on ads all over subway cars throughout New York City, he eventually became one of the hundred most recognizable New Yorkers.[7] Even though he did this mass transit campaign for thirty years, he said there was a big jump in his business the very first week after he started it.

Of course, if your big goal is to become a thought leader in your profession, then you would be aiming more to produce strongly-branded content, such as a book or series of videos, that demonstrates your expertise, and then find ways to get that content in front of the eyes of potential clients.

Whatever your current big objective, write it down now and continue with the next four steps in this process.

<u>Action Step #2:</u> Determine which qualities you want to be known for.

It can be frustrating when certain positive qualities you or your business possess, somehow get lost in the shuffle in terms of the public's perception of you. Perhaps you're a dentist who's invested a lot of time and money into upscale cosmetic dentistry, but is still mostly known as a professional that merely cleans teeth and fills cavities. Or maybe you're an entrepreneur who's recently earned an MBA in business, but who is still routinely dismissed as an intellectual lightweight.

This step allows you to take another crack at making your overlooked advantages an integral part of your Persona of Impact.

---

7. Billy Parker, "Dr. Jonathan Zizmor, The Subway Doctor," *The Gothamist*, May 8, 2009 http://gothamist.com/2009/05/08/dr_z.php

First, come up with three descriptors of the main positive qualities that people already ascribe to you – and then come up with three positives you'd *like* to see emphasized in your personal brand.

For example, let's say people already perceive these important qualities in your brand:

- Trustworthy
- Hard-working
- Friendly

But maybe you also want them to see these three attributes:

- Authority
- Innovative
- Professional

Think hard about your two lists of three and write them down – then move on to the next step.

Action Step #3: Define Your Persona

The next step is to combine these six words into three two-word phrases that reflect your desired persona. You'll end up with three new powerful concepts that can help define your Persona of Impact. By linking qualities you're already known for to qualities you want to be known for, you're creating a foundation of credibility to improve your personal brand.
For example, perhaps you might put together the two three-word lists we offered in Action Step #2 to create the following three combinations:

- The Independent Authority (i.e., you know a lot, but you're not compromised by corporate partnerships)
- The Hard-Working Innovator (i.e., you're creative and out-of-the-box, but not flaky or unreliable)
- The Friendly Professional (i.e., you get the job done, but you're also very relatable)

In each case, you're teaming up a known quality with an unknown quality – which validates the unknown.

Action Step #4: Create your Statement of Persona

In this step, you want to take the qualities you put together in Step #3 with the objective you named in Step #1 – then fill in the blanks of the following statement:

"I want to be known for being _____ so that I can _____."

For example, let's say in Step #1, your objective was to be a thought leader in your specific field. In that case, your Statement of Persona might read:
"I want to be known for being an independent authority, a hard-working innovator and a friendly professional in order that I can be seen as the leading expert in financial consulting in my community."

After you craft your statement, ask yourself the following three questions to see if you need to refine it:

- *Is this the personal brand that best represents who I am and what I can do?*
- *Does this personal brand create value in the eyes of my customers/clients and the community at large?*
- *Can I follow through on living up to this persona? Am I risking personal credibility?*

You may need to go through some back and forth to craft the best possible Statement of Persona, until it really resonates and you feel totally comfortable with it going forward.

Action Step #5: Road Test Your Statement of Persona

When you're happy with your Statement of Persona, it's time to see if others are as satisfied with it as you are. What you mainly want to look for, as you share the Statement with trusted friends and colleagues, is if it indeed accurately reflects who you are and what you want to accomplish.

It's no secret that many personal brands fail simply because they don't deliver what they promise. Can you live up to your own Statement? Are the words you use to describe yourself and your business accurate? This is the time to find out – before the public figures it out for you.

This process actually might uncover some stronger (and more obvious) qualities that you don't see in yourself; friends can often see us much better than we can ourselves. So don't skip this step, it's important to give yourself a reality check before launching any kind of Persona of Impact.

Of course, your personal brand will continue to evolve over time – so take yourself through this process at regular intervals, say, every other year or so. A Persona of Impact is not static; it grows and changes as you and your business grow and change. Make sure it keeps up with you as you continue on your journey to success.

About Nick

An Emmy Award-Winning Director and Producer, Nick Nanton, Esq., produces media and branded content for top thought leaders and media personalities around the world. Recognized as a leading expert on branding and storytelling, Nick has authored more than two dozen Best-Selling books (including the *Wall Street Journal* Best-Seller, *StorySelling™*) and produced and directed more than 40 documentaries, earning 5 Emmy Awards and 14 nominations. Nick speaks to audiences internationally on the topics of branding, entertainment, media, business and storytelling at major universities and events.

As the CEO of DNA Media, Nick oversees a portfolio of companies including: The Dicks + Nanton Agency (an international agency with more than 3,000 clients in 36 countries), Dicks + Nanton Productions, Ambitious.com, CelebrityPress, DNA Films®, DNA Pulse, and DNA Capital Ventures. Nick is an award-winning director, producer and songwriter who has worked on everything from large-scale events to television shows with the likes of Steve Forbes, Ivanka Trump, Sir Richard Branson, Rudy Ruettiger (inspiration for the Hollywood blockbuster, *RUDY*), Jack Canfield (*The Secret*, creator of the *Chicken Soup for the Soul* Series), Brian Tracy, Michael E. Gerber, Tom Hopkins, Dan Kennedy and many more.

Nick has been seen in *USA Today, The Wall Street Journal, Newsweek, BusinessWeek, Inc. Magazine, The New York Times, Entrepreneur® Magazine, Forbes*, and *FastCompany*. He has appeared on ABC, NBC, CBS, and FOX television affiliates across the country as well as on CNN, FOX News, CNBC, and MSNBC from coast to coast.

Nick is a member of the Florida Bar, a voting member of The National Academy of Recording Arts & Sciences (Home to the GRAMMYs), a member of The National Academy of Television Arts & Sciences (Home to the EMMYs), Co-founder of The National Academy of Best-Selling Authors®, and serves on the Innovation Board of the XPRIZE Foundation, a non-profit organization dedicated to bringing about "radical breakthroughs for the benefit of humanity" through incentivized competition – best known for its Ansari XPRIZE which incentivized the first private space flight and was the catalyst for Richard Branson's Virgin Galactic. Nick also enjoys serving as an Elder at Orangewood Church, working with Young Life, Downtown Credo Orlando, Entrepreneurs International and rooting for the Florida Gators with his wife Kristina and their three children, Brock, Bowen and Addison.

Learn more at:
- www.NickNanton.com
- www.CelebrityBrandingAgency.com

About JW

JW Dicks, Esq., is a *Wall Street Journal* Best-Selling Author®, Emmy Award-Winning Producer, publisher, board member, andco-founder of organizations such as The National Academy ofBest-Selling Authors®, and The National Association of Experts,Writers and Speakers®.

JW is the CEO of DNAgency and is a strategic business development consultant toboth domestic and international clients. He has been quoted on business and financialtopics in national media such as *USA Today, The Wall Street Journal, Newsweek,Forbes, CNBC.com*, and *Fortune Magazine Small Business*.

Considered a thought leader and curator of information, JW has more than forty-threepublished business and legal books to his credit and has co-authored with legendslike Jack Canfield, Brian Tracy, Tom Hopkins, Dr. Nido Qubein, Dr. Ivan Misner, DanKennedy, and Mari Smith. He is the Editor and Publisher of *ThoughtLeader® Magazine*.

JW is called the "Expert to the Experts" and has appeared on business television showsairing on ABC, NBC, CBS, and FOX affiliates around the country and co-produces andsyndicates a line of franchised business television show such as *Success Today, WallStreet Today, Hollywood Live*, and *Profiles of Success*. He has received an Emmy®Award as Executive Producer of the film, *Mi Casa Hogar*.

JW and his wife of forty-three years, Linda, have two daughters, three granddaughters,and two Yorkies. He is a sixth-generation Floridian and splits his time between hishome in Orlando and his beach house on Florida's west coast.

CHAPTER 6

TRAIN WRECK AT THREE MILES PER HOUR

BY MAX HOOPER, PhD

The snowflakes swirled around me, blown by a cold northeasterly wind. I looked down and could see ice-filled cracks in the highway next to my suitcase.

My walking gait was slow as I moved down the highway, holding up my thumb to try to catch a ride. Large truck trailers full of chickens flew by me at 60 miles an hour on their way to processing plants in the Ozarks foothills.

As the cold wind pushed me along, it was a time for reflection. On my own since age sixteen, now a year later here I was, but where was I going? Just an hour before, I was driving my old 1957 Chevy only to have it stall at a stop light in a small town. It was its final ride. A stranger helped me push it from the intersection to a gasoline station. The station owner gave me his review of the problem, I had no money for repairs so he offered me $100 for the car. I found myself walking from the station, down the highway with all that I owned in one suitcase and $100 in my pocket.

Introspection and reflection came easy as I was on the road for many hours. Some people would comment as I passed through several small towns, "Boy, you are going to freeze!" Others, "What are you doing?"

The truth was, I did not know what I was doing. I was just going and trying to figure it out as I went. . . a road to nowhere. It seemed like I was in a train wreck that was occurring at three miles per hour, slow, steady and destructive. The questions kept coming to my mind, "What am I doing? Where will I go? What will the future bring? What should I do?"

Many paths were possible for the people from my high school graduating class; college, military careers, or join the workforce. Life decisions lay before me, my resources were very limited and I really had no position or opportunities that I could try to maximize.

I'm really cold and it's getting dark. Approaching was a large truck, I could barely make out the brand on the side "Capitol Pride Meats." The driver slowed beside me, leaned over and opened his door. "You want a ride?"

"Yes, Sir!" I could hardly believe my luck, I was riding in a Big Truck with a heated cab and soft cushioned seats. A definite change of atmosphere and the kindness from a stranger changed my world in that moment.

The ride in the truck got me to the next large town. I was able to get a job and eventually decided to try college. At that time there were no college loans, but I was able to work multiple jobs to get through.

During this time, many ideas, and even dreams were sifting through my mind. One day I laid out on a piece of paper what I would 'love to do' if I could do anything in the world. Each of these wild ideas was similar in that they most probably could never be accomplished in my lifetime. Crazy, out-on-the-edge ideas for a young mind.

My high school graduating class voted me least likely to be alive at age 40, or something to that effect. So the idea of these big goals was really a dream more than any possibility of reality. Little did I know at the time that some of them actually would find life. Seven Dreams did emerge overtime, and it still amazes me each time I reflect on these thoughts.

DREAM #1

- Run and Finish the Boston Marathon.

This was a crazy idea considering I had never run before and did not play sports in high school or college. Additionally, I had never been to Boston or the East Coast of the United States.

DREAM #2

- Complete college and complete a Ph.D.

No one from my family had ever gone to college, much less had a college degree. My grades from high school were low average, and my classes were not college prep classes.

DREAM #3

- Family.

Growing up, my family consisted of my mother, father, sisters, a brother and myself. Family was important to me, though we moved yearly or even more often than that. A family to call my own, a place to settle and watch them grow, this was my dream.

DREAM #4

- Write a book.

Another odd thought in that I was not a writer, nor had any experience or skill in writing. In fact, I struggled to read through my school years. This really didn't make any sense because I was not a researcher or student of writing.

DREAM #5

- Global Traveler, seeing the world with global involvement.

My total travels to date amounted to several trips to a few surrounding states as my father's job changed frequently. Not much of a travel resume.

DREAM #6

- Start a company, grow it, take it Public, then exit.

I must have seen something on television about this process. There was no one that I knew that had done this and had only heard about it. It seemed to be a great adventure, seemingly impossible. But it energized me.

DREAM #7

- Successful life.

At a young age, having a successful life seemed admirable. I did not know exactly how to define 'successful life' or what that even meant.

Now, please remember that I was the least likely to accomplish these ideas and threw them out as paths of interest to follow. So what was my energy source? Over time it grew out of relationships with friends, mentors, family, circumstances, a lot of work, and prayer with the faith to persevere.

Ultimately, what I am about to share hasn't been easy. However, the results have been gifts to me. I'm hoping that they may inspire others to dare to dream.

MY DREAM OUTCOMES!

DREAM #1

■ Run and Finish the Boston Marathon.

The story is long and full of unbelievable events and circumstances. I was able to run and complete five Boston Marathons!! This led me to other events and over time allowed me to:
- Run 100+ Marathons
- Run over twenty 50 Mile and 100 Mile runs
- Run in Europe, multiple 50 K and 100 K runs
- Run the Sahara Desert in Morocco
- Run Pike's Peak Marathon fifteen times
- Run Grand Canyon eleven times
- Run across Death Valley to the top of Mount Whitney 146 miles
- Run Lake Tahoe 72 mile loop four times
- Run the Grand Slam of Ultra Running – Five 100 mile Ultras in one summer
- Run London to Cambridge 100K, London to Brighton 100K two times

Many more runs could be listed. I'm still amazed that this all happened, starting with such a crazy dream.

DREAM #2

■ Complete college and complete Ph.D.

When I finished college with a four-year BBA, I had the lowest grades that were possible to have and still graduate. Working three jobs in college allowed me to complete this goal. Great times, I was blessed.

The BBA was first, then an MBA, then a Ph.D. Eventually, five doctorate degrees were completed:

Ph.D., Th.D., D.Min., Ph.D. & D.Min.

Through my elementary school through high school years, my family moved several times a year. That being said, I had a varied and incomplete learning of the basics. I struggled with reading for many years and just assumed I was a slow learner. Imagine my surprise to find that I loved learning after I pushed my way through college. A life-long learner, interestingly I learned to study and follow my curiosity as it leads me through varied areas of interest.

DREAM #3

■ Family

This most joyous and Best Dream that came true is my family. My wife is my best friend and fellow adventurer. We have five children and seven grandsons! It's hard to believe as I think back to that frozen highway with only a small suitcase in hand, that one day I would have a home overflowing with love and meaning.

DREAM #4

■ Write a book.

Book writing was challenging for me. Where do I begin with no training or experience? I started with stories from marathon running and moved on to dissertations, essays and a foray into business investment practices. Some are:

- *Chariots of Pain*
- *Infinite Possibilities*
- *Containing Fringe Benefit Costs*
- *Distance Education Technology and Delivery Media*

- *Expository Studies – Psalms, Proverbs & Song of Solomon*
- *Driven* – to be published in 2017
- *Blockchain Enabled Applications* – to be published in 2017

DREAM #5

■ Global Traveler, seeing the world with global involvement.

Over time, interesting and diverse trips all over the world have occurred. Trips for pleasure, yes, but also for business, missions and global non-profit organizations. In 2015, I was honored to speak at the United Nations in New York. This year a trip to the United Kingdom is planned with study at the University of Cambridge.

DREAM #6

■ Start a company, grow it, take it public and exit.

Many companies were started and merged over the years. In one company that we started, my partners and I had never been in this type of business before. However, in little over twelve years we put together a portfolio of 110 television studios and broadcast stations, grew the value, and took it public on NASDAQ. I then was exited to work on other projects.

DREAM #7

■ Successful Life

Over time, my definition of a Successful Life has grown and matured. Experiences, life-long learning, Life Lessons comprised of challenges with both hard times and good times have helped me develop strategic thoughts and ultimately plans for action. There is a power that comes to you when you are weak, that pushes through circumstances and carries you forward.

Everyone has to define what a Successful Life means to them. I've taken all my life's experiences and distilled the lessons I have learned as keys for you on your life journey.

MY KEYS FOR SUCCESS IN LIFE

1. BE A GIVER
   God's loving kindness appears in the midst of both adventures and adversities.

2. RESPECT PEOPLE
   Everyone you meet has issues that they are dealing with. Be gentle with others.

3. DREAM BIG
   Have faith to believe your issues can be resolved, and your goals can be accomplished. "Perseverance wins the day!"

4. BE A GIVER
   "Give to Get." Think about the other person's position. Play Win-Win.

5. COURAGEGOUS PERSEVERANCE
   Search to find a way, when others think there is no way, and relentlessly pursue it to the end.

6. LOOK FOR THE BIG PICTURE
   Wealth Creation comes from many types of capital: financial, social, manufactured, natural and human—not just financial.

7. SEARCH OUT WISDOM
   Get counsel from many, then make your own decisions

8. LOOK FOR THE GOOD
   You can, if you think you can, using faith power.

9. PASS IT FORWARD
   Bless others as you would like to be blessed.

10. SHARE YOUR DRIVE
    Live to ignite and inspire God-sized outcomes in peoples' lives.

So, what projects are currently being worked on for 2017?

1. Writing two books.
2. Study and Research at Cambridge University in the UK.
3. Running a 100k run and a 100 mile run.
4. Launching multiple channels on our global capital formation engine, "Merging Traffic."
5. Capital raising on Cloud-based technology companies.
6. Projects using digital media in China and other countries.
7. Entrepreneur models created on FinTech, Blockchain, and capital formation.
8. Launch of StartUp Nations Ventures, a company that works on technology start-up companies in Israel.
9. Global projects with several global non-profit aid organizations.
10. More, more, and more …fun, excitement, and adventures.

My hope is that some of these activities and goals might inspire you to live fully alive, be fully "DRIVEN" with your impact to Bless others and make the world better because of your life's activities. The thoughts are summed up by Brendon Burchard in his book, *The Charge:*

> *Did I Live?*
> *Did I love?*
> *Did I matter?*

About Max

Max W. Hooper, Ph.D is the chief executive officer of Merging Traffic and Investment Banking lead at Triloma Financial Group. He is responsible for the company's management and growth strategy, serving as the corporate liaison to the financial services industry and various capital formation groups. Prior to starting the company, Max was co-founder of Equity Broadcasting Corporation (EBC) – a media company that owned and operated more than 100 television stations across the United States. Max was responsible for activities in the cable, satellite, investment banking and technology industries and during his tenure it grew to become one of the top ten largest broadcasting companies in the country.

Earlier in his career, Max was the managing partner of the #1 E.F. Hutton Financial Services office in the country for four consecutive years. Max has owned two Broker Dealers and a Registered Investment Advisory Firm [RIA]. Max is an author of several books and many essays on global, economic, and historical topics.

Throughout his career, Max's specialty has been debt and equity financing—having raised capital for a wide array of companies across the country. He has started multiple businesses in the areas of technology, lodging, internet and service industries. Additionally, he served as President of Mergers & Acquisitions for a national financial services company. Max has served on the investment committee of several venture capital and angel funds, and has completed "work out" transactions as a Certified Debt Arbitrator [CDA] representing banks and private transactions. Max is the founder of a global 'crowd funding' company that specializes in providing funding for "start-up" companies. Max is a Strategic Advisor for the Institute of Simulation & Training at the University of Central Florida, the largest University in the USA.

A lifelong learner, Max has earned five doctorate degrees: Ph.D., D.Min., Ph.D., Th.D., D.Min. from a variety of institutions. As an avid runner, he has completed more than 100 marathons and an additional 20 ultra-marathons, which are 50 or 100 mile runs. Max has completed the Grand Slam of Ultra Running.

Max is committed to his family and is a husband and father to five children and seven grandsons. He is active in many organizations and serves on various boards of directors.

Max works globally with several ministries and non-profit aid groups. Max was honored to speak at the United Nations in New York in 2015.

CHAPTER 7

TEN SUCCESS PRINCIPLES

BY STEVE & KELLY MCCARTHY

We are filled with joy writing this chapter as we reflect on what got us to this point. Life has really changed for us and we are now able to change the lives of others by helping them make the small changes that helped us get to where we are today. Seeing family members and friends use our success principles to better their lives is the second-best gift we have ever received. The greatest gift was the one that started it all for us. I think that would be a great place to start.

The gift of hitting the bottom! Sounds crazy, right? I will never forget how much hitting the bottom did not feel like a gift and I hope you are reading this from the bottom right now. I know that sounds terrible, but hear me out. At his lowest point, I was broke, terrified, rationing fish sticks, bouncing checks and completely ready to throw in the towel. I was too embarrassed to ask for help and went to work everyday pretending to be alright. One time in particular, I had been broke for months and finally payday was here. I was not only going to be caught up (back then meant not late on any bill) but I was also going to have $200.00 left over! On the way to work. . . flat tire! Broke again! I actually lost it and was a grown man in tears that night.

I awoke the next morning in complete anger at a little after 3 a.m. I suited up and ran to a nearby town. I ran angry for a good hour and stopped at Re/Max Gold. At that time, Re/Max was home to the great real estate agents. I had wanted to be a real estate investor/agent for a while but until that night I was waiting for things to happen. I thought there would come a time that would be perfect for me to start. I had been waiting for that day for years. That night, in front of Re/Max, I DECIDED that day was now. I VISUALIZED pulling up in my BMW, jumping out with a smile on my face, phone to my ear and strutting my successful-self right through those doors. I kept visualizing that day until I had that smile, the BMW and that recruiting call from Re/Max.

It took finally hitting bottom to strip away all of the fears and excuses of starting to live a better life. Everything from that day forward has always been easier than I thought and more valuable than I had imagined. It is always hardest to take the first step! With that I say again, I hope you are on your way up or even better – from the rock bottom of your life.

I had now decided what it was that I was going to do with his life. I was single and working as a mailman, a job that I had learned to hate. I was broke, tired and hanging on to the hope of a successful life when I finally took action. I had enrolled in real estate school. Little did I know, somewhere, about a week earlier, someone else had decided on the exact same path.

Kelly was working for a different Post Office and God knew just who I was waiting for when he sent her to help our office that day. I got lost her in her beautiful blue eyes for four long months and then we got married.

Kelly, like I did, before we met, had enrolled for real estate school. We both had the same goals of becoming real estate agents and investors. This was key to our success. Kelly is not living his dreams and I am not living hers. WE are living each others and we are living it purposefully. We had just combined households when we sat down together and decided what our life together would look like. We completely disregarded where we were, what we had, what people would think of our goals and what would be realistic. We picked where we wanted to live, how we wanted to live and how much money it would take to get there. We then reverse engineered what it would take to get there – all the way down to daily activities. We review those goals every day and every night. This little goal-setting process has kept us focused on the big picture, allowed us to double our revenue each year, and allowed us to leave the comfort of our safe government jobs after three short years.

We worked our Postal jobs during the day, but at night we really put in work. I would love to say that it was easy and 'get-rich-quick' is the way to go. That is not our story. We were grinding day in and day out. No days off. I remember our first real estate deal, a million-dollar home in a town where no home had sold for that yet. I was negotiating the first offer, at the Post Office, on break, hoping my boss did not come calling. Kelly was at her office begging her supervisor to print out the offer to present to our client after work. We did everything we could, every day, until we built the business up enough to quit the jobs we hated and pursue what we loved. When you really know what you want, eliminate the excuses. . . you will always find a way.

In our business and in our marriage, success is a priority. If you pick the right partner, it is easy to succeed. You must have someone who is aligned to your goals. When you both are heading in the same direction you are able to feed off of each other's drive and motivation. Your partner must be strong in the areas that you are weak. I love people, I hate details and I hate paperwork. Kelly loves details and data. Its perfect! Your partner can connect with people with whom you are unable to. In our business, we each have clear roles and responsibilities. We hold each other accountable to them. This is something that our coaches insist we do and we succeed when most partnerships fail because of it.

The greatest advantage we have over most of our competitors is the people we surround ourselves with. We studied investors, sales experts and top real estate agents through audio books and podcasts, 8-10 hours a day, while working our day jobs. Now we are lucky enough to sit in the same room and learn from some of them. Mentors and coaches shave years off the learning curve, and it's imperative that you get the best ones you can find.

We may never reach a point in business where we are satisfied with where we are and that is alright with us. It's the growth in our business and as a couple that we find happiness. We are however, doing what we love each and every day, and we get to do it together!

We wish you the best in your journey and hope you create a life you love. To help you get started, here are our Ten Success Principles to help you go from your job you hate to successfully doing what you love:

1) ***Know what you want to do.***
   If you are doing something you love, it never feels like work. Every single time we have an opportunity to help someone in real estate, we light up. We get fired up and cannot wait to get after it. It is what we love. If you love fishing....go fish! Find who makes a living fishing, do what they did and you will earn a living, just like they did. Is it going to be easy? No! If it was, everyone would do it. Is it possible with hard work? It's a fact that it is possible because people are already doing it. You just have to put in the work.

2) ***Decide and then take action.***
   It is always hardest to take the first steps. All of the doubt creeps in and you begin to fall back on society's rules, your parent's advice and what the world says we should do. If you do what everyone else does don't be surprised if you end up where they are. Reach up and take advice from those that live like you want to live, and decide to take action.

3) *__Learn from those who are where you want to be.__*
Someone has been where you are and gotten themselves to where you want to be. Learn from them and you may find short cuts to success.

4) *__Find the right partner.__*
By finding the right partner you are free to focus on what you are great at. You will be able to avoid doing the tasks that don't produce the highest dollar return in your skill set. Choose a partner that is strong in the tasks that you are weak in and you will always pull each other up. The wrong partner will pull you in the wrong direction and keep you in constant conflicts.

5) *__Set clear goals and revisit them daily and nightly.__*
We set our goals with a fun, exciting process. We write a letter to ourselves. We write this letter as detailed as possible, as if everything in the letter has already happened. We write how great life has become because we hit our goals, we lost 'X' number of pounds, we vacationed at so and so island, we helped 'Y' number of real estate agents learn the business and changed their financial lives, we sold 'Z' number of houses, gave 'X' number of dollars to our church, etc. These goals are always so ridiculously big that we can not even imagine how we will accomplish them. We read our letter every day and every night. There is a great podcast on this process we learned from Sean Terry at: flip2freedom.com. This is an amazing podcast and we highly recommend it.

6) *__Reverse engineer your goals. -- 10 year, 5 year, 1 year, quarterly and finally the daily task.__*
We take our 10-year goals and break them down. Where do we need to be in five years to achieve the 10-year goal? We next look at where we need to be in one year to hit our 5-year goal. Then again, where do we need to be this quarter to hit our 1-year goal? Where do we need to be at the end of today

to hit our quarterly goal? Then we decide what one thing can we do today, really well, that will help us hit our daily goal. Do this one thing every day, as if it was as important as breathing, and you will blow your ridiculous goals away.

7) *Set rules and responsibilities for each task.*
You and your partner must have agreements in place that allow you to clearly define what each of you are responsible for. Who is doing what task? It is crucial that each task moves you both towards the goal.

8) *Hire a coach.*
When we started, we thought we could not afford a coach. We know now that the thousands of dollars we wasted or lost in life lessons could have been spent on a coach that would've protected us from those mistakes.

9) *Do what makes you uncomfortable.*
We have found the further we move out of our comfort zone, the more success and opportunities come into our lives. When we try new things, we always get different results.

10) *Always do the right thing.*
We believe doing the right thing always leads to a better long-term results. We would never go against our values for a short-term gain. We believe that doing the right thing, no matter what the cost, always has long-term benefits. It gets back to people when you fix a problem, or make an honest suggestion that might be to not buy or sell with us right now, and *people recommend people they know that they count on.* In a referral-based business like ours, your reputation is everything.

About Steve

Family has always been the most important thing to Steve McCarthy. His parents, Steve and Debbie, were his greatest role models. Steve's dad taught him that everything was about working hard and being reliable and honest. On the other hand, his mom made sure he knew to be kind to everyone. Above all, both of them instilled in him the value of family. They made family dinners a priority, and were very involved in their kids' sports, coaching them both on and off the field. Growing up, they learned to do anything to help a family member, a friend, or even a complete stranger.

In 1997, Steve started working for the United States Postal Service. It was a steady job, and one that he really enjoyed at the time. While working at the postal service, he started a small mechanical business with his future brother-in-law. As a mobile fleet service, they would go out to companies with large fleets and work on their vehicles. They did well for two years, but ended up selling the business, simply because it was safer to stick with the post office.

Safer was what he thought he needed for himself at the time. But one day, a co-worker lent him an audio disc full of highlights from books by authors and motivational speakers like Tony Robbins and Robert Kiyosaki. Listening to them made him think for the first time about developing himself and investing in his future, rather than just working for somebody else until retirement. He couldn't get enough. He searched for more books by each author, started reading them one after another, and found himself really wanting *more*.

It was a true turning point in his life. As much as he enjoyed his job, he knew then that he needed to do something bigger, and he decided he wanted to get into real estate investing. Living paycheck to paycheck wasn't going to allow him to buy a lot of property, though, no matter how much he studied the business. So, he resolved to earn his real estate license in order to get started in the field and put away some money.

He continued working at the post office during the day, and he was lucky he did, because that's where he met Kelly. Though they had met each other a few times as kids, they didn't really reconnect until they started working together. She really is an incredible woman: assertive, intelligent, beautiful, and an amazing mother to their children. Kelly came from a background of similar family values, and they've carried those into their daily lives today.

About Kelly

Just like Steve, Kelly McCarthy learned a lot from her own family. On her mom's side, her grandparents were business owners, running a local Goodyear store. Very hands-on, they worked sixty-hour weeks, from open to close. She admired their incredible work ethic, and really tried hard to mimic it. Her dad's parents, meanwhile, taught her a lot about working at home. They lived next door to her family, and she learned a lot from them, they were very kind and generous, and she strived to be like them as well.

She got her first job at Bishop's Pumpkin Farm in Wheatland at age fifteen. From then on, she was always working, whether it was managing some local video stores or putting in time at a Ford dealership in town. She got her job at the Post Office in 2005.

She bought her first house in 2007, and shortly after, the market took a dive. Suddenly, it was worth about half of what she paid for it. While so many others in the same situation became afraid, that experience actually sparked her interest in real estate investing. She already knew she loved the experience from when she purchased her own house, so she figured she could repeat that process and find an exciting, rewarding career in it.

It was difficult to get started, as she had to do a lot on her own to provide for her kids. She didn't know if she could do it at first, but she became 'way more motivated' after meeting Steve. Together, they had a support system.

Steve and Kelly are the perfect combination. They complement each other's strengths and weaknesses. They both earned their licenses in 2012, and they've been a team since day one. Although they originally intended to focus on investing, they found immense fulfillment in helping others achieve their dreams of homeownership, and it quickly became clear that they had found their true calling.

CHAPTER 8

THE MOST COMMON MISTAKES ENTREPRENEURS MAKE WHEN STARTING AND RUNNING A BUSINESS

BY ISAIAH COLTON

If you have ever started a business or considered starting a business, you most likely have heard the discouraging statistics about how most businesses fail within their first five years. According to a recent article in *Inc. Magazine*, only 4 out of 100 businesses survive past the ten-year mark.

So, when I started out my first venture in 2014, I wanted to make sure that I was not one of the statistics. I set out to maximize my chances of succeeding in business. I am a huge personal development junkie, so I searched for the answers from some of the most credible sources that I knew. I studied the big names like Brian Tracy, Tony Robbins, Chet Holmes, Jay Abraham and Mike Koenigs among others. I also hired Jim Tegeder, a seasoned business veteran from the Entree Network as a consultant. Jim helped me find models that I could use to make sure my business started on a path for success right out of the gate. I painstakingly studied and applied ideas over and over until I would get the result that I was looking for. The first year or so was hell on earth. I made so many mistakes. At one point, it got so bad we had to move out of our beautiful 2,700 sq. ft. house into a small apartment and fell almost 3 months behind on our mortgage. Over the next several months though, I started integrating the ideas that I learned more effectively and seemingly overnight everything started to fall into place. By the end of the second year the business had turned a strong profit, and by the end of the third year we experienced over 400% growth! Since then we have started up five other businesses all of which have been profitable within their first year.

Just this past summer while playing golf at a private course, Locust Hill Country Club, I started reflecting on the past few years. I recalled all the crazy stories, including undependable employees, vendors not following through, product trial and error and all the stress on my family, and I said to myself. . . **I never want anyone else to go through what I went through, EVER!** It was at that moment I decided to compile and document the system we used to go from $0 to $20 million in just over three years with very little start-up capital. That documented system is now called the *Ultimate Startup Formula*. The key objective of this system is to identify the "most common mistakes" business owners make, and how to avoid them.

What we found is that these principles are largely universal – regardless of the industry or type of business. Avoiding these mistakes will either help make or save you millions of dollars as they have for me.

As an example, here is a selective summary of issues to be considered prior to starting and running your business:

Mistake Number 1:
- Not conducting a Self-Assessment before you start the business.

A lot of consultants will tell you to start out with a strong business plan as your first step. While that step is important, it's not the first step. The first step is to have what my mentor used to call a "come to Jesus" meeting. Meaning, do an honest analysis of your strengths, weakness, abilities, funding capabilities, connections, time commitments and any other factors like family and support that could affect the outcome. I was asked to speak about entrepreneurship at a local college and this was the first point that I made to the audience.

Most people make the mistake of being so enamored with their idea that their head goes in the clouds and they don't think these basic things through. While you don't want to limit your thinking, it's important to first just be real. What are you willing to give up - time, money, other sacrifices? Do your gifts and talents complement the business you're in? Is your significant other willing to support you through whatever may come your way?

Hopefully, you can see how important it is to think these things through even before you start your business plan or invest in your company. After you've hammered all that out, then dive into the business plan. By taking this approach, you will find that you can start building the plan around the real circumstances facing you, instead of hoping that your circumstances fit the business plan. The latter sounds almost like playing the lottery. . . you can win sometimes, but let's be real, most of the time you lose.

Mistake Number 2:
■ Not making serious and honest assessment of partnerships.

Every entrepreneur faces the decision to proceed with partners or to go it alone. Both tracks are fraught with critical obstacles and risks. Even so, this decision is often given the least amount of in-depth thought and analysis. There are undeniable benefits of having the right business partner by your side. The operative word being the "right" partner. If the choice or selection of a partner is flawed, it not only does not add value, but more often leads to frustration and destroys the execution of plans and results. Careful consideration must be given in advance to sensitive areas involving equity, control, employment, contracting and possible separation. All partnerships must be carefully assessed.

To reiterate, the right strategic partnership can be the basis of great success, but the wrong one can destroy everything. Don't get caught up in the excitement of the business and just take on any partner with no forethought. I learned this the hard way after we caught a business partner stealing from the company. Fortunately, I had a strong contract agreement that made it easy to remove the business partner from our company. I had another partner who was not pulling his weight so he would have reaped tremendous financial rewards simply by leeching off my hard-won success. Again, I was fortunate to have the right agreement in place to sever the relationship.

Mistake Number 3:
■ Not developing an effective Time Management System

Seriously? You're asking yourself. How did time management make it into the top 10? I can tell you, the time management system we have built in our organization has measurably contributed to our success and financial gains more than any other process. Every employee in our company follows a time management system that helps them plan their entire month, week, day and hour to maximize productivity.

I heard Mike Koenigs say at one of his recent seminars, "Money loves speed, and time kills deals." When I first heard this quote, I almost fell off my chair because of its simple but powerful truth. Everyone in our company has a plan, takes action, gets feedback and then goes back and takes action again. A "Ready, Aim, Fire and Review" approach. Time blocking is a key to our ability to operate this way. *The Ultimate Sales Machine* by Chet Holmes and *Eat that Frog* by Brian Tracy are two great resources to help you come up with your own Time Blocking System. I time block everything, I mean everything. In the *Ultimate Startup Formula*, we show you exactly how to use Time Blocking to help your business grow with balance, even when you go through hyper-growth stages.

Mistake Number 4:
■ Not developing an effective training system.

If you look at any great company, a major reason they are so great is because they have great training. They plan for excellence and then train to it so they don't leave anything to chance. One of the best example of a great training business is right here in my backyard, that business is Paychex, Inc. The business has grown into a multi-billion dollar company and if you ask the employees what made them great, they will all tell you, it was the training. They had a unwavering commitment to develop and implement the best training program for their employees so their clients would experience great results.

Most businesses are just flying by the seat of their pants. The small business owner gets really good at what they do, then goes on to hire their first or second employee. Oftentimes the owner becomes extremely frustrated because the new employee can't do the job as well as he could, so he blames the employee. The reality is that it's more likely the new employee was given a brief "overview" then was expected to magically have all the skills needed to operate at full proficiency. If you actually think about it, this approach, while common, is so far removed from reality – it's mind boggling. Document everything, train every day, and watch your business grow.

Mistake Number 5:
■ Failure to truly articulate a compelling value proposition.

Every entrepreneur has in their mind the benefits of their product or service. They assume the gifts they offer to the world are valued and self-evident. The problem is that often that assumption is faulty, and based upon incomplete analysis and research. One representative example of this can be seen in a 1998 case study of Pets.com. It seemed that selling pet products online even at that time was a slam dunk winner. Millions of dollars were spent successfully on building awareness, but the model failed due to a lack of consumer interest and action. There was no perceived value in getting pet products delivered to homes. Had Pets.com actually done some research they would have known this in advance. Pets.com did not offer a compelling enough value proposition – there was simply no market requirement for home-delivered pet food.

It is valuable to consider that nothing happens until you sell something. Making the sale is dependent on the perceived value received by the buyer. The formulation of that proposition is critical, and should be well defined in advance of writing plans or moving forward. And unless you want to be the dreaded "me too" product, you'd better explain how you're different. The great thing is you only need to start off with one unique value and promote it relentlessly. Don't try to do too many things at once. Find one good thing and make sure everyone knows about it.

Mistake Number 6:
■ Failure to maintain focus.

A common factor in failed startups is the lack of focus. Many great business ventures have been taken off course by distractions. The appeal of new ideas or "a better way" can overload an already resource-constrained business that doesn't have the financial or human resources to execute them. Trying to do too many things means you do nothing well and spend too much time dealing with crises.

Entrepreneurs should take the time to conduct extensive research into which business model they should adopt for their company before launch. And once you have settled on the best model for your company, stick with it, as changing models while your startup is already up and running will only hinder your success.

This doesn't mean businesses shouldn't pivot as needed in accordance with market realities. Change is inevitable but any shift must be carefully considered and tested as to its impact on the base model and organization. This principle also applies to managing employees. Non-productive performance or activities not aligned to the business model should be eliminated immediately. As you become successful be cautious about expanding your product lines, or divisions too quickly - you want to avoid the mistake of stretching your resources and compromising the very thing that made you successful in the first place.

"The most important thing for startups to do is to stay focused, because there are so many things you could be doing. One of them is the most important. You should be doing that. And not any of the others."

SUMMARY

Prior to writing a single word of a business plan, entrepreneurs should immerse themselves in the world of pre-concept definition and analysis as described above. The odds of success will be enhanced, there will be a boost to your self-confidence and your battle plans will be fully internalized. The final business plan and financial model will be based upon more dependable assumptions as well as a thorough risk assessment including the appropriate measures to manage them.

Future opportunities for employees and team development along with comprehensive training can be defined and structured as a part of the business plan. That process is further described in the *Ultimate Startup Formula* from **Advantage U.**

The strength of your business model will be evident from your ability to speak to all of the various pre-concept issues and your thoughtful analysis of each. You will reinforce your own belief in the vision and bolster your commitment, resolve and burning desire to succeed.

About Isaiah

Isaiah Colton is an Entrepreneur with a strong skill-set in Sales and Marketing. He has a passion for taking ideas and turning them into profitable business ventures. Being brought up by a hard-working farm family, he developed a powerful work ethic. Pairing that strong work ethic with a Generation Y mindset, Isaiah recognized that it was possible to combine hard work and integrity with working smarter.

After spending 10 years in senior sales management, Isaiah brought together a team to build a startup business, called **Advantage U** – Home Sellers Resource, focused on helping home sellers achieve their goals and finding better ways to connect with the best real estate agents in their market. The idea came from Isaiah's own experience struggling to find an agent and facing the results of working with the wrong one.

That emotional, time consuming and costly experience convinced him that there had to be a better way. In less than three short years, from 2014 to 2017, Advantage U exploded from 1 employee to over 100 employees and is approaching $20,000,000 dollars in sales volume, servicing thousands of home sellers across the country. The best part of all was that he did this with just a few friends and family members investing their time, money and energy during the critical early stages of the company.

Isaiah and his team have also been recognized by some of the top 1% of agents in the country many of whom are on the *Wall street Journal's* Top 250 list. These top agents recognized the team for using Power Branding techniques to create a new source of business, and helping them expand their presence and brand within their markets.

Along the way, Isaiah and his team started several other companies using the same proven business techniques now known as the *Ultimate Startup Formula*. This is a step-by-step process to start, grow and become extremely profitable very fast with the least amount of headaches and risks along the way. Isaiah's goal over the next five years is help thousands of new Entrepreneurs and other Professionals start their own businesses or advance their careers. The ultimate goal will be to demonstrate that one can be successful with integrity while changing people's lives for the better in the process.

The *Ultimate Startup Formula* from **Advantage U** provides proven methods and techniques for that process.

For the full list of **The Most Common Mistakes** and a turnkey system to help your business thrive visit: www.ultimatestartupformula.com.

Dedication

This is dedicated to my wife, family, colleagues and employees for being my driving force and a critical part of my success.

CHAPTER 9

WHY DID I STUMBLE PAST THE POINT OF NO RETURN?
LEADING THE FUTURE OF HEALING

BY JOHN PARKS TROWBRIDGE MD, FACAM

But ... __death__ was a known and listed risk. K.W. had suffered with painful, limiting arthritis pains in the past few of his 53 years, and no prescribed medications had helped. Desperate, he saw another new physician. "A drug has come out that might help – Let's try it." Sudden relief from the shackles of continuous pains thrilled him and his wife. The doctor felt deep satisfaction ... until weeks later, when he was called to the Intensive Care Unit across the street. Despite forcing unit after unit of blood into his veins, K.W.'s pressure steadily fell, dimming hopes of taking him to surgery 80 feet down the hall.

Watching him slowly die crushed the nurses – *and* the doctor, in his first year of general practice. The depression that set in lasted for months. He finally decided to go to law school or business school, close his solo practice, and focus on public policy medicine behind a desk, maybe at the National Institutes of Health, where he had trained.

Perhaps you have guessed that the doctor above is ... *me*. Sure, the risk of bleeding and death from **any** prescription *or even over-the-counter* anti-inflammatory pain and arthritis drug is well known, including "low-dose" aspirin, non-steroid "NSAIDs," and *all* cortisone-type medications. NSAIDs are the most widely-used medications in the world, now *Number 5* on the list of Top 10 Most Dangerous Drugs.

Medication-*caused* ulcers and other gut bleeding from NSAIDs kill many thousands of Americans yearly, a documented "side effect" in each drug brochure – not to mention their major risks for heart attacks and strokes, and much more. What are the chances? About one hundred percent, if it happens to *you!* Who ever expects to be the victim?

Known side effects – all potentially suffered by the *patient* not by the doctor. Perhaps, I thought, I misunderstood what really needed to be treated. My drive to avoid contributing to such losses was intense. What follows are some of the secrets I discovered. I resolved to find and design safer ways to help patients, following the time-honored caution to physicians-in-training: "First, do no harm."

I will forever remember that the signature on his prescription was *mine*. Unexpectedly, by the grace of God, I soon discovered my answer: the phenomenal power of **natural healing methods** to reverse and even cure many problems that cripple us, steal our vitality, and even cause our death. *I had stumbled past the point of no return.*

☐ NOW[1] you can easily help your doctor help YOU better – www.doubtyourdoctor.com/driven/drug-side-effects

Finally Healing With Nutrition Where Drugs Had Failed

Biology or health classes in school share no hint of how "processes" work inside our bodies. Simple fact: each "part" is made from foodstuffs, they provide the nutritional "pieces" (amino acids, essential fats, minerals, vitamins) that are rearranged to construct all of our organs *and* to repair them when damaged. Unless … the pieces are *missing*! I *had* to rescue Robert from a peg-leg future.

Amputation made sense as the only choice … to his doctors. Robert enjoyed his motorcycle almost more than anything else in his 28 years – until the accident that almost ripped off his right leg. He came to see me 15 months later, his lower leg supported by a posterior splint (half a cast). He spent almost 13 months in the hospital. Repeated operations "cleaned up" his gaping wound, but various procedures failed to reunite the bones. Robert's raw tissues kept "spitting" splinters of bone, and he refused every insistent recommendation for amputation.

The key: eating hospital food for a prolonged period was a shortcut to nutritional deficiencies and failure to heal. Simple testing showed massive shortage of minerals. I knew precisely what supplements he needed for repair – and his bones mended

[1]. I am thrilled to share how you and your family and friends can **find easy answers** for a healthier, more active, more rewarding future by reviewing exclusive checklists, reassuring articles and booklets, easy home health hints, delightful patient experiences, and links to informative audios, videos, books, and websites available at each ACTION ITEM link in this chapter. *Even better* – you can freely propose these resources to your personal physicians, exceptional nuggets of knowledge "off the beaten path" so they can easily learn and offer these impressive treatments to all their patients.

as usual in just over 4 months.

> Correct diagnosis is critical. Correct treatment is essential. Find it *now* – Fix it **right!** Because ... health is your greatest wealth.

As a birthright, each of us receives the priceless gift of a self-healing body. Unaware of the consequences, we easily trade it for a bowl of porridge called "drugs and surgery." Then we complain "that don't taste right." How could you activate true healing? *That* was the start of my journey on the path of natural healing.

Early successes with *safe* and *effective* "nutritional medicine" convinced me that 4 lecture hours in medical school were not near enough. In 1985, I earned a Diplomate in Preventive Medicine for master's level studies in nutrition. A key lesson: healthy repair is a *science* that *can* be learned and practiced with elegance.

> ☐ NOW you can easily help your doctor help *YOU* better – www.doubtyourdoctor.com/driven/healing-with-nutrition

Toxic Metals Are Killing Your Heart! *(and More)*

> *In the 15 minutes while you're reading this chapter:*
> 21 Americans will suffer a heart attack, 3 of those will have an unexpected first attack – 11 will die, almost all of them out of the hospital.

Then more will suffer and die in the *next* 15 minutes – and the *next* – and the *next* . . . . .

Another trip to the E.R. and I could be dead! E.W. didn't look or act as old as his 50 years, but vitality was seeping from his life due to nine "small" heart attacks: progressive muscle damage stole his energy, he couldn't walk more than five minutes, worrisome pains came and went, and he was helplessly watching his business fail. The surprise was how quickly he began to improve with reducing toxic metals (such as lead, mercury, arsenic, cadmium, others) through an FDA-approved treatment called "chelation therapy." Strength and stamina returned but his conventional doctors had promised "You have to get used to suffering, that's just a fact." Then his chest pains simply ... *disappeared.* After just a year of treatment, he joyfully resumed fulltime work.

Now 17 years later, he excitedly shares, "I'm almost back to a pre-heart attack wellbeing." Quite a testimonial to the profound power of natural healing when factors **blocking** your healing are removed, when factors you need are **missing** and are finally provided, and when **"switches"** such as hormones, oxygen, and others are "flipped on."

> Correct diagnosis is critical. Correct treatment is essential. Find it *now* – Fix it *right!* Because ... health is your greatest wealth.

He limped in with just a flicker of hope in his eyes. Life had taken a brutal turn for J.S. as he struggled every day in the last several of his 74 years. Worsening blockage in his legs and feet meant operations, drugs, and mediocre results. Amputation was looming. His cardiologist just shook his head as he documented deteriorating blood flow every 3 months.

He wandered across from their parking lot to my building. "Well," I began, "we've successfully treated folks looking far worse than you, and many even older. Chelation reduces toxic metals, even though heart 'specialists' aren't familiar with the treatments, doubt they're safe, and don't believe they produce results naturally."

His hopeful enthusiasm quickly blossomed into unbeatable

conviction as he was walking farther and faster on feet that felt normal and legs that were stronger. His bragging to the nurses performing circulation tests wasn't necessary – the tracings were *proof-positive* and they insisted that their doctor "come see!" His cardiologist just nodded ... and *no*, he didn't send *any* of *his* patients for *my* care.

Talk about opening my eyes! I barely contained my excitement 35 years ago when learning how to diagnose and safely reduce toxic metals – *I had found Ponce de León's "Fountain of Youth!"* Conventional physicians and regulatory agencies are *dozens* of years behind the advancing knowledge. My lectures in Taiwan, Brazil, Canada, and Mexico are far better received than in the United States, where unjustified intolerance, prejudice, and even prosecution have been the norm since the 1960s.

Personal pollution by toxic metals over a lifetime is stealthy and goes undiscovered, undiagnosed, and untreated because conventional doctors stop asking "Why?" about 5 questions too soon. Drugs are "stoppers" or "blockers" (*anti*-histamines, *anti*-acids, *anti*-hypertensives – prescribed by **anti**-doctors?) that interrupt chemical reactions causing distress. Toxic metals interfere far more. Our world is more toxic every year. Patients see "organ" doctors (heart, gut, skin) who ignore sneaky poisoning ... so *your* health worsens by the day. Makes sense to treat the *cause* not just the *complaint!*

☐ NOW you can easily help your doctor help YOU better – www.doubtyourdoctor.com/driven/toxic-metals-choke-blood-flow

You're Poisoned By Elusive Infections No Doctor Sees?

It's just heartburn – but those drugs never help me. Years of testing and prescriptions from "wonderful medical specialists" meant D.R. was desperately suffering. Her newest "acid-blocker" wasn't any more special than many before ... and it didn't help any better, either. What astonished her (and her skeptical engineer husband) was how effortlessly her detailed *history* revealed chronic *fungal* overgrowth sapping the comfort from her life. Within weeks, every day became a joyful experience, just like years earlier: "better and better, amazing ... no headaches, no nausea ... energy and stamina is increasing so nicely ... I was so sick and weak, I am not now ... I am getting a good night's sleep, none of that awful back pain in the morning ... You saved me, no kidding ... [my husband] can see a big difference in my quality of life." Oh, her reflux and belly pains? Gone. Quickly.

> Correct diagnosis is critical. Correct treatment is essential. Find it **now** – Fix it *right!* Because ... health is your greatest wealth.

Imagine my wonderment in 1983, realizing how common yeast infections were connected with extraordinarily differing symptoms and illnesses – in up to *40 percent* of patients! In 1986, Bantam Books published my continuing bestseller, *The Yeast Syndrome*[2]. *Localized* yeast infections (athletes' foot, vaginitis, thrush, chafing skin, dandruff, and so on) are easily treated. Recurrent or *persistent* conditions signal a deep-seated *syndrome* with *"harmless"* yeast *overgrowing* in your gut,

[2]. Here's a laugh: Reduction of sugars and starches is essential, so *I* developed the "MEVY" diet (Meats-Eggs-Vegetables-Yogurt) in 1984, the same year I taught my good friend Doug Kaufmann how to diagnose and "treat yeast." As a Med Tech, Doug needed to work with (and *educate!*) interested doctors. He learned well and began writing wonderful books. While videotaping in spring 2016 for his syndicated TV show, *Know the Cause*, I asked Doug, "Why did you 'steal' my diet program?" "Did I steal it?" "Kinda looks like it, Phase I and so on." "Sorry about that, didn't mean to ... But I have story for *you*. Several years ago, some fellow called to ask if he could 'steal' *my* program. I said sure ... but what for? He said 'I want to call it the . . . . . *paleo* diet!' I thought, 'Well, what a crazy name.'" Now trademarked by Loren Cordain, "Paleo Diet" is the leading buzz on the internet. *I will take my bow now.* (P.S. – I still like my MEVY program better.)

generating severe problems. Unseen and unsuspected, they percolate toxins that are absorbed along with your foods. These substances journey throughout your body, *poisoning* chemical processes everywhere. (Secret: yeast are dedicated to making a *Happy Meal®* out of *you*.)

Many *young adults* "mysteriously" suffer discomforts and outright illnesses ... first in one system, then another, the next, and so on. The Yeast Syndrome does not always show "outward" signs while creating devastation inside. "Elegant clinical testing" involves keen observation. Without expert diagnosis and care, fungus problems *always* lead to unnecessary drugs, operations, and even death. Conventional doctors are wearing blinders, referring patients to one "organ" specialist after another.

From some of my sickest patients, testing shows conclusive evidence in the blood: *plant* fungus. We find these "weirdos" in MS (multiple sclerosis) *and* in heart blockage plaque *and* elsewhere. An avenue for odd fungi might be the mouth, slipping along the gums to the roots of the teeth then into the general circulation.

"Normal appearing" teeth with infected root-tips deep in your jaw can harbor dozens of nasty bacteria – also documented in the "plaque" blocking heart arteries in those very *same* patients! And we're finding *plant fungus* **in** those deposits. Treating other unsuspected/silent *parasite* infections can restore comfort, vitality, even life itself. (We "worm" our dogs, cats, horses, and cattle – but *ourselves?*) Don't overlook "volatile organic compounds" (gases, VOCs) in buildings and vehicles, making your immune system vulnerable to *all* invaders.

Hey! Bacteria, parasites, fungi/yeasts – they *cannot* exist in blood without killing you quickly (sepsis). *"Old school!"* We need to rethink our "rules" in light of cutting-edge research. Reminds me of the drunk leaving the bar, crawling on his hands and knees, looking for his car keys on the corner ... when he last remembered having them "down the block." When asked why he wasn't looking over *there*, he replied, "Because the light is so much better over *here*."

You ***don't think*** about what you ***don't know*** about or you disbelieve, you ***don't test*** for what you don't think about, you ***don't treat*** what you don't find, and you ***don't help*** patients whose diagnosis you ***simply missed.*** . . often for years, even decades. "Close" counts only in horseshoes, hand grenades, and shotguns.

    ☐ NOW you can easily help your doctor help YOU better – www.doubtyourdoctor.com/driven/yeast-syndrome-suffering

Seriously? *Complete Relief* From Suffering "24/7"?

The drive back from San Diego was brutally painful. J.T. dove into the motel pool and his low back pain was sudden and severe. Alarmingly, his legs wouldn't kick: could he struggle to the side and pull himself out of the pool? His friend drove 500 miles back home with him writhing in pain in the back seat of the VW Beetle. The orthopedic surgeon slapped films on the x-ray viewer: "If I didn't know you were 21, I'd say these changes were in a 70-year-old man."

Ligament laxity syndrome (inherited disorder causing "hypermobile" joints) spans a wide gamut with perhaps 10 percent affected, mostly women. Most people with "mild" forms don't know unless diagnosed with scoliosis. J.T. had a moderate undiscovered case with a straight spine. Twenty years later, a freak accident caused severely pinched nerves, requiring cleanup of a ruptured low back disk. Suffering like many "lax" patients, he underwent not one but two operations for his lower *neck*. Happily he avoided "fusions" that set the stage for worsening degeneration and later operations. Each procedure gave immediate relief of pain.

Most importantly, he discovered an advanced form of prolotherapy, unusually safe natural injections (*not cortisone!*) to stimulate strengthening of stretched/torn supporting tissues in his neck and back, shoulders, knees, eventually *all* of his joints. As with about 90+ percent of "prolo patients," his pain relief and functional recovery was outstanding. Like many others with arthritis or most sports injuries, surgery was *not* the right choice for most of his joints. Full disclosure: J.T. is ... *me.*

I'm surprised that you still have a shoulder! D.P. enjoyed unexpected results with "prolo" to his complex ankle injury – and asked whether his shoulder could be helped. Tic-tac-toe scars betrayed several extensive operations, last one involving major reconstruction. The 4-page "op report" was impressive – and because of that surgeon's expertise, he *still had* a shoulder that could be treated with healing injections. Almost unbelievably, the 54-year-old finally recovered *full* strength and function.

Your knee injury is severe – Playing soccer again is possible – but ... "Grabbing life by the horns" was how it always was for G.R., both work and play. A national-champion level soccer player for many of his 38 years, his knee injury cut short his hustle, despite aggressive operations. "Can you get me back to intensive play?" After exam and assessment, I replied "Probably, *but* you won't like the intricate treatment needed." "I didn't ask whether I'd *like* it, just can you *do* it." After dozens of exacting prolotherapy sessions, he enthusiastically returned to a couple more years of extreme performance and many more of daily comfort.

Correct diagnosis is critical. Correct treatment is essential. Find it *now* – Fix it ***right!*** Because ... health is your greatest wealth.

(Secrets: MRIs are rarely necessary for joint problems. Cortisone never helps joints heal. "Rooster-comb" gives comfort but rarely strength.) *"Standing"* regular x-rays show sagging effects of gravity.) Rarely do neck or back problems require surgery – same for virtually *all* other joints. Knee "scope 'n' scrape" operations have been challenged as providing no better result than … *doing nothing.* (Except they get you closer to your next scope and then finally "joint replacement.") Patients (inaccurately!) told they have "bone-on-bone" and need "new plastic and new steel" often improve dramatically with prolotherapy instead. Results in virtually any joint can be long-lasting and spectacular: *Get out of your pain and get on with your life!*

☐ NOW you can easily help your doctor help YOU better – www.doubtyourdoctor.com/driven/no-daily-drugs-no-surgery

Unbelievably … A *New* YOU!

You're kidding, right? Relief of hip pain you've suffered for 40 years? E.B. was happy with the prolotherapy injections helping his knee – and he asked about treating his hip. Quarterback in high school, an onrushing opponent "nailed" his right hip with his helmet. White-lightning pain! Then lingering pains and limitations for 40 years. "I would like to try a unique 'cellular allograft' (stem cell) preparation that I think might help." Injection into his hip was easy and pains disappeared. Where the helmet hit was far different and much more serious, a tissue compression injury (RSD) … and *that* pain took a week to disappear.

Six months later, he stepped backwards off his hay-baler (*oops* – no step there!) and fell onto – you guessed it! – his right hip. Days later he came in: "This hurts like before; should we try more cells?" "*Wait!* – this is a separate new injury. Let's see how you recover. Assuming all goes well, that's confirmation that your earlier treatment was a success." His pains *disappeared in a week*, and he continues to enjoy usual activities like he had *never* seen in his adult years.

Correct diagnosis is critical. Correct treatment is essential. Find it *now* – Fix it *right!* Because ... health is your greatest wealth.

As variations on so-called "stem cell" treatments become more mainstream, just what they are and how they heal is important to understand, to best treat degenerative diseases. When special "allograft" tissues (not your own stem cells) are used, the source *must* be a trusted one: a federally-registered tissue bank is the one I depend on, exceeding my expectations in how these youthful cells are isolated, processed, and safely preserved.

I routinely witness impressive results "all over" ... not just for my patients but also for *me*, personally. This rich source of cells and essential growth factors promotes regeneration of joint support tissues and reduces inflammation. I nickname this unique preparation as "the package that performs." *Because it does!*

☐ NOW you can easily help your doctor help *YOU* better – www.doubtyourdoctor.com/driven/miracle-of-healing

What "They" *Won't* Let Me Share With You Now!

Deadly – This heart recovery simply <u>couldn't</u> be true! M.H. was stunned by the news: idiopathic cardiomyopathy (heart muscle enlarging and weakening ... but doctors can't figure out why). In his early 30's, he was willing to do "whatever," but results were always disappointing. Some 8 years later, he started taking an obscure botanical concentrate. After only 2-½ months, his heart performance registered "normal" on the tests, with heart inflammation apparently resolved – and he remains *well* some 3 years later (still taking the plant elixir!). And *that's* just *one* of our "secret potions." We're dazzled by emerging supplements, herbals, and other "concoctions" to assist detoxification, reduce inflammation, and achieve improvements never before available.

We're heartbroken that I just can't get pregnant. Over the past 39 years, I've been blessed to treat over a dozen women with "fertility difficulties" to conceive and bear children. The number could be many more ... but regular doctors stuck on "high-tech" approaches never refer for other procedures. Personalized pregnancy nutrition (starting *months* ahead) and programs to support robust breast milk have rewarding outcomes. *Most* "female" problems – PMS, period issues, menopause, even polycystic ovaries and more – are easily corrected by safe and simple approaches, sometimes including elegant and convenient hormone replacement. Even osteoporosis (weakening of bones) can be reversed to *"normal"* without the advertised drugs that can kill your jawbone ... among other nasties.

The older I get, the more I struggle trying to lose any weight! Obesity is the scourge of our time, including pre-diabetes (Metabolic Syndrome) tumbling toward deadly heart attacks and strokes. The "food pyramid" is a joke, a mistake that will crush you like a bug. The best way to control weight and worry – not about blood sugar, cholesterol, and triglycerides – is to avoid sugars and starches, eat meats and lots of crunchy vegetables, and enjoy regular walking and exercise. Alarming fact: "statin" drugs are dangerous and their value is challenged. Another secret: Statin drugs kill yeast! (Maybe *that's* how they produce any benefits!) An essential key: thyroid hormone function must be carefully balanced for energy, better health, and weight control – and *not* by misleading blood tests.

YOUR mind is a dreadful thing to waste. *All* aging is a *disease* happening one day at a time. "Senior moments" are one thing, early dementia is altogether worse. Consider this: aspirin or Tylenol® can "treat" any fever, but that's just a fancy Band-Aid® aimed at the *complaint*. What is needed (for *all* "mental" *and* physical problems) is targeting the *cause* of the problem.

Failing organ functions with diabetes, cancer, headaches, chronic sinus and lung infections, high blood pressure, congestive heart failure, blocking arteries, macular degeneration vision changes, sleep apnea, gum inflammation and degenerated teeth, dysfunctional mouth ("jaws too small for your tongue"), even "trivial" constipation, "heartburn"/reflux, and a *zillion* other afflictions often go poorly treated (sometimes even *missed*) due to overlooking the root causes.

This should be obvious: if you want to completely heal a blister, stop wearing the offending shoe! More than a dozen "alternative" strategies can *improve* autoimmune disorders – rheumatoid arthritis, lupus (SLE), psoriasis, ulcerative colitis, Crohn's colitis, MS (multiple sclerosis), and *over 70 others* – without resorting to TV drugs offering dreadful side effects.

The list of simple or complicated distressing symptoms and illnesses goes on and on, based on thousands of patient successes over my career.

Admitting a hidden agenda: I help all kinds of doctors to <u>*teach each other*</u> *how to better care for you!* One unique distinction is that I am the *only* professional ever to serve as president, officer, director, and advisor for two of the most influential professional organizations in the integrative healthcare field: one in *medicine* and one in *dentistry*. My years of leadership positions, hundreds of lectures, several books and major articles, dozens of CDs and DVDs have given me a broad background of all aspects of healing. From that vantage, I **easily** share "the bigger picture" on the development of diseases (and effective treatments) in *every* organ system, persistence of fungal and other infections, spine and joint degeneration, and inflammation patterns that lead to suffering and death.

***Why* won't they let me share more with you here?** These stories and hundreds of others, many just like yours ... seems the book covers limit how many pages I can grab! Take advantage of clear explanations and easy, effective, practical advice and referrals on the link below.

☐ NOW you can easily help your doctor help *YOU* better – www.doubtyourdoctor.com/driven/make-me-well

Past the Point of No Return: *Life* Celebrating *Health*

Correct diagnosis is critical. Correct treatment is essential. Find it *now* – Fix it *right!* Because ... health is your greatest wealth.

The lessons in my practice are inspiring: Opportunities are available right now for both you *and* your personal physicians, where your focused commitment to insist on better, to discover better, to do better, and to be better **can and will** produce many of the improvements you seek. Avoid frustration: never try to educate someone who *resists* knowledge at all costs. Just say "You're fired!"

The only way to find new solutions is to challenge the ones that exist. Especially where the final answer offered is, "There's nothing more we can do – You have to learn to live with it." *Not so!* You already know how to live *with* it, you want to live *without* it!

As a caring and curious physician, I was blessed that I "stumbled" early in my career. I have been driven to blaze a trail for patients *and* their doctors, leading to distant horizons of exceptional results with both *medical* **and** *health care.* The secrets to "doctoring" are easy: a singular motivation to study intently the emerging sciences, to seek many details from your patients, to ask probing questions then listen intently, to perform competent hands-on exams, and to order and understand advanced tests that unlock the secret causes of inflammation, toxicities, deficiencies, and failing functions … so that they can finally be corrected – rather than once again merely bandaged.

Once past the point of no return, never, never, never give up.
When life is your choice, failure is not an option.

About Dr. T

What turns a bright-eyed eager Cub Scout into an adult driven by passionate dedication to achieve worthy goals? Should we want each of our children to be so motivated? In 105 years, only 2 percent of eligible Scouts have mastered the tasks for the highest honor: Eagle Scout. Fewer have earned a bronze palm, been honored as Order of the Arrow, performed as Junior Assistant Scoutmaster. So what?

Eleven of the twelve Apollo moonwalkers were Scouts, two were Eagles. Most astronauts were Scouts as teens. Advancing ranks in Scouting inspire higher levels of planning, preparation, and skill toward specific, definable goals. Early years of directed effort foretell a tireless commitment to strenuous training, vital in selecting astronauts (and physicians).

Happily, Dr. Trowbridge ("Dr. T") enjoyed early affirmation when selected as a National Merit Scholar and California State Scholar. At the National Science Foundation Summer Biology Program at the University of Texas as a high school senior, he was fascinated with intensive inquiry and research. In his education, he was privileged to relish and embrace the exceptional standards of a half dozen Nobel-winning professors. Working as an assistant in immunology and microbiology during his studies at Stanford imparted the value of exacting research, day after day. His curiosity at Case Western Reserve Medical School inspired a dozen videotapes on congenital heart disease for cardiology education.

Political efforts as the first At-Large National Trustee of the American Medical Student Association allowed his appointment as liaison to several physician boards. His keynote address to the American Podiatry Association and backstage advocacy led to a "meeting of the minds" with the AMA. Three years later, podiatrists previously barred were finally welcomed into hospital operating suites. As chairman of the board of the National Health Federation, he restored financial stability to expand education programs and lobbying for freedom of choice.

A patient tragedy from prescription medication spurred Dr. T to discover safe, natural solutions producing spectacular results not seen in conventional practice. Drawing on his foundation as an Eagle Scout, his commitment is not merely to exceed but to excel as a world-class practitioner. His innovative discoveries combining effective medical/surgical technologies with classic-but-overlooked healing knowledge and novel scientific breakthroughs are recognized in over five dozen volumes of *Who's Who*.

Encountering patient problems beyond his skills, he sought other techniques … then set about to upgrade them! A Master's in Nutrition proved essential for his expertise. *The Yeast Syndrome* (Bantam Books best-seller) introduced millions to a clear path to better health. Dr. T's expertise in treating desperate patients suffering with unsuspected toxic heavy metal poisoning is praised by his colleagues. Lectures around the world, books, and articles have shared his perspectives and patients come from far and wide. Honored as a Fellow of the American College for Advancement in Medicine and for Distinguished Lifetime Achievement by the International College of Integrative Medicine, he reflects with deep appreciation for his parents' unwavering encouragement on his path to Eagle and beyond. How has his singular drive for achievement evolved? Look soon for eye-opening revelations in his forthcoming series of *Doubt Your Doctor*™ books.

To contact Dr. Trowbridge:
- www.healthCHOICESnow.com
- DIAL 1-800-FIX-PAIN
- www.doubtyourdoctor.com/driven/my-story

CHAPTER 10

MOVE UP TO CONDO PROFITABILITY

BY JOSEPH PAZCOGUIN

Everyone knows that owning property is a "money pit."

And it's not just the down payment and mortgages. There are always so many additional costs and losses once you buy a piece of real estate! There's maintenance, prevention, general depreciation and illiquidity. Real estate ownership is rewarding for sure, but it always requires so much financial risk and exposure!

Or does it?

What if I tell you that there's a way to buy property with other people's money, and to do one neat little trick to change everything about the value and potential of your real estate?

No, I'm not just talking about "flipping." Flipping houses is great, and it works. But it's a crowded field. Most of us have seen one of the dozens of home improvement shows focusing on it — it's the trendy, straightforward practice of buying distressed properties, 'amping up' their appeal, and selling them at a premium to a discerning buyer who appreciates the low-hassle solution of buying a house that's just been thoughtfully renovated. And the before and after nature and high emotions always makes for great TV!

I'm talking about something that you won't see on TV shows. It's a little less flashy, but the upside is enormous. And best of all, it's a wide-open field that isn't overrun with competitors!

I'm talking about condominium conversion. As a Southern California-based design consultant and third-generation construction industry professional, I've learned a lot about meeting — and monetizing — a public need for housing. Everyone needs a place to live, and in the flashy Los Angeles area, everyone *wants* a nice place to call home! But even in other markets, what I'm about to tell you can be leveraged to fulfill the universal human need to put down roots.

My company is called **Apartment to Condo**, and those two things are the essence of what we do. It's a bit complicated when you get into the details, but the concept couldn't be simpler.

Let me tell you a story.

First, some background. What do you think of when you hear the word "Hollywood"? For people all around the world, "Hollywood" stirs up images of glamour and mystique. It's got the cache of the Academy Awards, not to mention the prestige of all those classic films that its studios put out. Hollywood is "Tinseltown" — or the "City of Stars," to use a more recent reference!

But for Los Angeles residents, "Hollywood" called to mind a different image. For the past couple of decades, the area had become congested and crime-ridden. The neighborhood had a problem with violence and homelessness.

For many tourists who came to the area, the difference was quite stark. Hollywood is home to some of the most iconic buildings and monuments in all of the United States — for example, the Chinese Theatre, the Hollywood sign, or the Roosevelt Hotel. But for the past decade, Hollywood Blvd. has been filled with vagrants, filth, and pushy costume characters.

As you probably know, neighborhood reputation plays a huge role in property values. For many years, Hollywood properties were on the decline. As more and more people moved to Los Angeles from out of town, many rented an apartment in Hollywood. They did this because, as out-of-towners, they didn't know about Hollywood's reputation for seediness.

So, this created a cycle where Hollywood became more and more crowded with low-priced, high-density units. And the units became more dilapidated, as landlords were receiving a steady stream of renters. There was no incentive or need to "mess things up" by renovating or in any way updating the old buildings.

But I saw a business opportunity. Sure, it was great for these landlords and property owners to have a consistent stream of renters (and income). But like all great business opportunities — it's not about how comfortable your present situation is. It's about seeing the potential of the future.

This was my plan, for Hollywood and for many more places all around Los Angeles. At Apartment to Condo, I help clients convert rental dwellings held by a single owner into individual condominiums, saleable to different owners. And the key to my technique? I use other people's money to buy property — that way, it's all upside!

Let's take a closer look at this in action. A client may come to me when he is seeking to purchase a large dwelling. Maybe it is a multi-unit building, or a duplex or triplex. Remember, we're trying to think of property buying as a way to *make* money while enjoying the benefits of ownership.

If the client comes to me before he has bought or made an offer on a property, then I try to obtain pre-approval from the city beforehand to convert this dwelling to individual parcels in the future. One important key at this step is in understanding the applicable rules and limitations regarding zoning and permitting.

This is the power of pre-planning in action — it can save so much time and headache if you are able to anticipate your obstacles before they come up. This is one of the rare cases where, unlike that saying — you want to cross a bridge *before* you get there!

If we can obtain pre-approval to sell the dwellings as individual units in the future, then every step we take is geared toward that end goal. At my firm, I help with everything involved in planning, purchasing, permitting, and getting a property ready for its conversion.

That last category is enormous. I'm blessed to have a talented team of people who don't mind wearing many hats — and I like to wear a lot of hats myself!

What goes into condominium conversion? The better question may be, what *doesn't?* Remember when we talked about flipping houses earlier? Though condominium conversion is a bit more complicated, it follows all the same principles. Basically, you want to anticipate the end-user's comfort and desires.

What are the pain points of the person who will be living in (or renting out) these converted condominiums? Sounds pretty straightforward until you realize that answering that question involves a lot of hypotheticals.

For example, let's think back to a neighborhood like Hollywood. Before the area started becoming upscale, people moved to Hollywood because it was cheap, central, and convenient.

Obviously, when you start putting yourself in the shoes of

someone who would live in a converted condominium, the needs and desires are much different. An apartment is a place to live; a condominium is a place to grow.

So, when I look at properties that have formerly been rental units with my clients, we think about the ways that a condominium dweller approaches his living space in a totally different way than an apartment renter.

A condominium dweller is an owner, or even an investor. He probably wants to "future-proof" his home as much as possible, with structure and gadgetry that not only works well, but looks nice, too. He also probably wants to feel pride when he has guests over, and to feel secure in knowing that his place has good resale potential. For these needs, we direct our attention toward interior design, color work, furniture, and landscaping, to name just a few.

Remember, we want everyone who experiences this property—from the client making the purchase all the way down to the secondary renters who may live here in the future if the client seeks passive income—to feel that it is thoughtful, harmoniously designed, and pleasing to spend time in.

Using these simple tricks to add value to the property with thoughtful renovations to its structure, function, and appearance – and then to sell each individual converted condominium for $900,000 each after only three hours on the market. That's a total of $2.1 million in profit – and the original purchase is made with my client's money, of course!

My greatest goal is always how to add value for my clients. I know that when I make thoughtful, life-improving changes to their property, they will think of me each time they enjoy them.

Bonus: If they think of me when they visit the bank and find that their balances have grown thanks to the rental income, long-term profitability, or equity of their lovely new converted condo!

In condominium conversions, I have found a special niche of real estate that allows me to use my strengths to help others. I am studying to be a lawyer now, so that I may help my clients better understand the legal and zoning issues of their ownership.

I believe in streamlining my business in every aspect. By using other people's money, and relying on my trusted team of skilled specialists in every project — these are just a few of the ways that I preserve my mind and resources in order to help most people.

When I'm not converting condominiums, I am heavily involved with multitude feeding — a special type of faith-influenced charity in which we serve the most needy and the least fortunate. Faith and a passion for providing good service have been the compasses of my life — if I feel confused about my direction, I stop to consider how I can improve in either of those areas.

HOW DOES CONDOMINIUM CONVERSION HELP BUYERS AND COMMUNITIES?

As I've explained, condominium conversion is the practice of buying otherwise-zoned dwellings and preparing them (and securing the proper permits) to have them as condominiums.

Why do this? Who does it help?

1.   Condominium conversion helps the buyer

Obviously, there's a huge chance for resale upside. When a buyer spends his hard-earned money on a property that is eligible to be converted into a condominium, he is making a very wise investment in the space. Condominiums attract an entirely different rental clientele than apartment units. My clients love the increased freedom and control that comes from owning their property, and having it zoned as a condominium.

2.   Condominium conversion helps the community

I briefly discussed Hollywood's history as a somewhat run-down, lower-scale neighborhood. If you've been to Los Angeles recently, you know this is no longer the case! Builders have poured tons of money into the most densely populated areas of Hollywood. Now, you can find an Equinox gym, a brand-new W Hotel, and beautiful neon-lit facades right on the corner of famous Hollywood and Vine intersection.

An influx of investment into a neighborhood is good for everyone involved. In Hollywood, as in so many other improving areas that I have helped to convert condominiums in — increasing ownership rates in a neighborhood has a positive impact on lowering crime, improving facilities, and more. Condominium conversion helps to improve neighborhoods, and everyone who lives there benefits.

3. Condominium conversion helps the city

As someone who is intimately familiar with zoning ordinances and permitting rules, I can tell you that condominium conversion is great for the city! It brings them fees and adds to the responsibility and scope of their work.

4. Condominium conversion helps the construction industry

I have many capable employees and partners in all kinds of industries. Just think of every specialty that goes into home renovation — from electrical experts to gardeners to house painters — and you have an idea of the different jobs that condominium conversion can help directly and indirectly create!

5. Condominium conversion helps you!

In my experience, I have concluded that there is no bad time to do a condominium conversion. (Provided one has access to the capital, the time, and the proper counsel to do so, of course. Regarding the first point — don't forget to use someone else's money!)

Condominium conversions have the key benefits of:

a) Making property ownership more attainable for more people
b) Raising individual property values in a neighborhood, which can have the direct and indirect effects of improving people's commitment to "greater good" resources like schools, parks, and libraries
c) Increasing investment into local businesses by providing work for contractors
d) ... and more

Condominium conversion — in my somewhat biased opinion — is a no-brainer. Who doesn't want to make money, improve the community, and secure the long-term potential of their investment?

About Joseph

Joseph Pazcoguin pulled his first diploma out of a fire.

That's no exaggeration. As a child growing up with four other siblings in Quezon City in Manila, Philippines, Joseph was taught about the value of time early on. When Joseph graduated kindergarten, his mother told him that his precious time was best spent working hard, not on reading books. Working at a job would make him money; studying was just a frivolous pursuit with no immediate payoff. That was when she threw his diploma into an open fire.

But Joseph had a sneaking suspicion that he could pair the two — study and hard work — in order to create something that was greater than the sum of its parts. The moment he pulled that charred diploma from the flames, Joseph dedicated himself to being not only a hard worker — but an educated one.

This unique approach is the key to Joseph's company Apartment to Condo. Based in Los Angeles, Apartment to Condo is a full-service consulting firm that handles architecture, planning, permitting, landscaping, surveying, engineering, and interior design.

Sound familiar? Well, there's one key difference with Apartment to Condo. . . *Studying!*

Joseph brings three lifetimes of experience to each job he does. He is a third-generation design consultant. Joseph learned the construction business from his father, who learned it from his father before that. By studying what has worked over time — and what hasn't — Joseph is able to be smart about how he invests his time and money.

For Apartment to Condo the best use of time and money is a unique niche that Joseph created by himself. By studying the economic trends and financial shifts in the Southern California real estate market, Joseph realized that there was a little-discussed, highly lucrative field just waiting to be explored. It perfectly addressed the needs of a growing, increasingly upscale demographic, while also providing an irresistible investment opportunity for visionaries who believed in the obvious potential of Southern California real estate.

What is this win-win situation? It's condominium conversion. As a consultant/developer/planner/designer, Joseph and his team handle the logistics of permitting of multi-unit rental dwellings with sole ownership into separately-owned condominiums with individual ownership.

What does this mean in plain English? Well, for example, Joseph helped his client buy an existing four-unit apartment dwelling for $1.5 million with pre-existing approval to convert to condominiums. By adding value to the dwelling by modifying its engineering, structure, and general appeal — Joseph helped the client sell the entire building (now four separately-owned condos) for a total of $3.6 million, in 3 hours.

Apartment to Condo works with high-end clientele and people who recognize great potential upside. Their projects are all over Los Angeles, in some of its nicest enclaves, including Beverly Hills, Palos Verdes Estate, Manhattan Beach, and more.

Joseph is actively involved in giving back to his community through charitable works. He is deeply dedicated to "multitude feeding" — the practice of helping others when they need it most.

You can connect with Joseph at:
- planandpermit@gmail.com
- http://www.besta2c.com/

CHAPTER 11

FROM ZERO TO THE TOP

BY GEORGI GUNCHEV

People don't like to make mistakes, BUT...

. . . my experience shows me that the best way to learn is: first to try and second, to learn from mistakes.

. . . my experience shows me that the natural path to success is via mistakes and failures.

Why? Because my success is a direct result of my failures and mistakes. Because of that, I found out in practice, key techniques that work flawlessly anywhere, anytime. My key techniques are based on natural forces, on natural dependencies. This gives them strength and a powerful method of action. These techniques led me to the top. I will share with you three of my key techniques.

Let me tell you a story. I was asked to teach a man who was about to be dismissed. This man had worked for twenty years in sales in many companies and for one year at our company. All these years he had mediocre results. His last year was deplorable, awful. Practically, he was close to dismissal. Then I was asked to try to teach him my techniques and my way of work. After one year of training and collaboration with me, in January 2017, for a single month, he received a sum equal to his previous salary for

15 months. In fact, the amount was over 15 times more. How did this magical transformation happen? What is the reason?

I will share with you some of my key techniques and way of work. There are three of my key techniques in which I trained him, and which are part of the answer and are the part of the reason for his unbelievable success:

My First Technique:
<u>JUST CALL AND ARRANGE A MEETING</u>

In our industry, insurance, and especially in sales, all people agree that one of the greatest difficulties and one of the most frustrating points is the phone call. I mean when we call the prospect to arrange a meeting with him.

I continue. At the end of the first month since this man (his name is Slav) and I started to work together, after a phone call in which I set up a meeting with a potential client, he asked me a surprising question: "Do you ever receive 'No' for an answer?"

At the moment he asked me, I realized that he never seen anyone say "No" to me on the phone. I convert every telephone call into a meeting.

. . . And then I went back in time, to the beginning of my career, when I pretty often received "No" for answer.

At that time, I didn't know what to do to avoid the answer "NO." I had a product that was extremely useful for those people, but I couldn't explain it to them on the phone. I wanted to meet them, but they were not willing to meet with me.

How could I tell them how important and how useful my product was for them?

The purpose of the phone call is to "sell" the meeting, not to sell the product on the phone. And then I began to wonder how to talk to people so that they cannot refuse? How not to allow them the opportunity to refuse? And I asked myself:

- What is the nature of the process?
- What actually is happening?

And I put myself in their shoes. Here is what I thought:

From somewhere and somehow, I receive a call from a stranger, who talks some nonsense and wants to see me. What is my reaction? What do I think in this moment? – "Damn, I don't know this person. He talks some crap to me and I don't want to see him!"

But because everyone finds it much more difficult to reject such a request directly, even to the unknown person, it is much more convenient to start to ask questions to justify and confirm the decision which is I have already taken:

- "Where did you get my phone number?"
- "What are we going to talk about?"

. . . and this is the beginning of the end. This will end with "No."

At the beginning of my career, I was asking myself: "What is the natural process?" And the answer to this question led me to the top and over it.

In fact, if I want a meeting, but I can't explain why, then I will fall into a situation to try to "sell" over the phone, and this leads to a "No." I must tell them something that they are or will be interested in, or I have to do it according to an algorithm—so that they have no other option except to tell me "YES."

And here the innovation is - an algorithm that produces a result, a meeting. I call the prospect and directly tell him what I want to do, and I give him two options, which are: "Yes" or "Yes." It maybe sounds crazy, but I'm calling on people who are owners and CEOs, people who have done business from the start of their careers. What kind of people are they?

They are people of action. They had achieved something because they acted. I offered them exactly the same thing – action. Briefly and clearly, I tell them that I want to see them, give them two options, and ask them to choose the more convenient option. Actually, what I do on a subconscious level is I tell them I'm like them, I'm a man of action, and I clearly tell them, "I am like you and I want to see you."

And what does he or she answer? – "OK." What does he or she think subconsciously or consciously? What are they thinking? . . . "He's like me and I will see this man."

In fact, here is the innovation: I don't offer a service, I don't suggest a benefit, I don't sell them – I use something much stronger. I give them a message on the subconscious level. Every single person who is successful has the instinct to gather with other successful people like him. People buy from people they like. All successful people know that success goes through other successful people they know.

This is the reason why I and my team receive the answer, "Yes." This is the reason, why one year later, Slav sets up meetings with CEOs and owners of companies, and one year later he has an enviable income – he received in one month an amount that exceeded his previous salary 15 times.

The Second Technique:
HOW TO GET CRUCIAL INFORMATION

When we work with corporate clients, there are two things at play: one fact and one question.

1. This fact is: – there is fierce competition, because the bigger the customer is, the more our competitors want to work with them.
2. The question is: – "How do we win this deal?"

So the main question that faces each salesman is how to gain more information to be able to make the best offer to win a contract.

What happens is that everyone is trying and hoping to get crucial info; everyone is hoping to take a look at the client's old insurance policies and old contracts in order to be able to make the winning proposal. Naturally, anyone who says, "Give me your old contracts and I will make a better offer." receives a total rebuff. Even before completing the sentence.

And then, I asked myself a single question: What must I tell him so that he gives me all possible information I need, even the old contracts? Obviously, if I say, "Give me your insurance policies," they will not give them to me.

So I constructed the following approach:

Once we have completed the standard approach – building a rapport, identifying needs, and so on – I turn to the client to tell him:

"Mr. Customer, we, the insurers, work with documents. To be able to make you the best proposal, we need information." (Notice! I didn't say best or lowest price. I said, "the best proposal.")

And here is a crucial point: after the last word "information," I need to shut my mouth until the moment the customer starts to talk to me.

The customer already trusts me, he believes that I can give him the best proposal. What is the customer thinking at this moment?

'I like this guy, I trust him and he wants to make me the best proposal. With that proposal, I will be best protected and it will be most useful to me.' He pauses, . . . 'What does he need?' . . . 'He needs information.'. . . 'He said documents.' . . . 'What documents can I give him?' . . . 'Well, I have insurance policies. Actually, it is best for me to give them to him so he can make me his best proposal.'

And what do we hear? The customer says to us: "Okay, so what must I do? I can give you all the policies that I have and you will do the rest? Am I right?" Then I answer: "Yes, right."

Because we now have the necessary information, we can make the winning proposal. Each word is very well thought out and can't be replaced. Here again, natural laws work in our favor. We say something logical, we give him information in a logical sequence and the customer makes a logical conclusion/answer. I never tell the customer what to do. I want him to tell me that he will do what I want.

So, using this technique, Slav is achieving brilliant results, he is winning deal after deal and customer after customer, thanks to two simple sentences and the pause afterwards, thanks to this key technique.

The Third Technique:
THE MAGIC SALE

"The magic sale" is when the customer firmly and resolutely tells us that he will buy. And now, everyone who was ever involved in sales will say, "George, great! But this does not happen every time! This happens, but rarely, very rarely, and this is a pure luck."

I agree. And for me this outcome was rare and for me, it was luck. Until I make it purposeful. Let me explain. . .

From beginning to end, I lead the conversation. So finally, I have in front of me a man, ready to buy – a man who has no need of further persuasion on my part – who tells me, "I want to buy!"

How did I achieve that? Simply and easily.

Every product or service has benefits. We, as salesmen, know these benefits very well, don't we?

The formula is:

(1) Describe the benefit.
(2) ASK: Does he like this benefit?
(3) ASK: Will he use this benefit?

When the prospect answers "Yes, "Yes" and "Yes," then IN FACT, we have already sold them.

We describe simply and shortly, benefit #1.

■ We ask the prospect: Is this useful for him?
■ We ask the prospect: Will he use this benefit?

After that, we describe benefit #2.

■ We ask the prospect: Is this useful for him?
■ We ask the prospect: Will he use this benefit?

We do this for every benefit which the product brings to the customer.

At the end of the presentation, we have the following:

The prospect answers to us for every single benefit – "This is useful for me." and "I will use it."

Then the sale just happens. We do not have to persuade the

customer to buy, we have no worries about closing the sale. Our customer has already purchased the benefits of the product and he has said several times that he likes it and that he would use it.

With this technique, we solved a major problem at the end of the meeting:

- Will there be a sale?
- Will the customer buy?

The customer has already bought ... We just have to prepare the documents.

What do we have? We have a happy customer and a happy salesman. Someone from my team – for instance Slav – is this salesman.

After 20 years of hard work and poor results, and after a year of training with me, he told me: "For a first time since I was young and I started to work, for this Christmas and this New Year, I have no difficulty deciding what presents and so on to buy for my kids and for my family." He deserved it. He is a good student. Finally, he has dazzling success.

About Georgi

Georgi Gunchev started in Insurance and sales with AIG Life Bulgaria in February 2001. In the next two months, March and April, he reached the highest premium income and the biggest sales, even larger than the entire premium of the biggest sales managers with a sales force of more than 20 agents. Immediately spotted by the management of the company, in the next month he begins to conduct training, and he was the only agent invited to conduct trainings.

Trainings are made up of initial training and sales training for Agents and Sales Managers. Georgi doesn't lead the training using standard methods employed by the company. He develops his own methods of training, and the trainings have great success. The company reported that he has the highest results in initial training, compared with the results of other trainers. His sales training for existing agents and managers record the highest attendance, almost two times higher, as compared with attendance for training led by other managers and trainers. With the highest premium income for 2001, at the end of the year he led the rankings in front of the #2 and the #3 by several times.

In 2002, he again had the highest premium income, even with six months in the army (at that time, military service in Bulgaria was mandatory). In 2003, he started in Allianz Bulgaria, and after his first six months, he emerged second in Bulgaria, and forty-fifth in Europe, in premium income.

Professional challenges sent him to work with Luka Dokov – a legend in Insurance in Bulgaria and abroad. (Luka Dokov was one of the world's fifty insurance specialists as recorded in the Lloyd's of London Directory in the 1970s.)

Georgi then began work at a newly-created company, which first received a license for health insurance in Bulgaria. Of course, he achieved the largest premium income. In fact, virtually the entire premium income of the company for the first six months was due mainly to his work.

Subsequently, he worked for a year for Peter Schiffer – again in direct sales.

From July 2011, Georgi returned to insurance in Bulstrad Life Vienna Insurance Group. Although he had only six months of sales in 2011, he achieved the largest premium income for the year. Georgi had the highest premium income in 2012, 2013, 2014, 2015 and 2016.

Georgi is a member of The Bulgarian Psychological Society and The National Association of Experts, Writers & Speakers (NAEWS) in the USA. He is also a member of the Professional Speaking Association (PSA) in the UK and Ireland.

Georgi strongly believes that his mission is to share his experience and knowledge.

You can connect with Georgi at:
- georgilgunchev@gmail.com
- https://www.linkedin.com/in/georgi-gunchev-84857582/
- www.twitter.com/@georgilgunchev
- www.facebook.com/georgi.gunchev.1

CHAPTER 12

RISE AND SHINE

BY DARICE JORDAN

Tip #1: **Let that cry out**

The reason why many people do not cry is because they think that crying makes you a pitiful weak person who lacks confidence, but you can be confident knowing that when you cry to the Lord, he will answer you. And you can expect your tears of sorrow to turn into tears of joy when you don't give up.

- *A strong person is not the one who doesn't cry, but the one that sheds tears for a moment and gets back up to fight again!* ~ Wosheka Jefferson-Burriel
- *Crying doesn't indicate that you're weak. Since birth, it has always been a sign that you're alive.* ~ Anonymous
- *They that sow in tears shall reap in joy.* ~ Psalm 126:5
- *Have a good cry, wash out your heart. If you keep it inside, it'll tear you apart.* ~ Holytimz

Crying can be a healthy thing to do especially after a heart break. Studies show that crying reduces stress, lowers blood pressure and removes toxins.

- *Where you are right now doesn't have to determine where you end up.* ~ President Barack Obama

Tip #2: **Detoxify**

Detoxifying your body can help improve your health by removing toxins that slow it down, so can detoxing from toxic people. If you're feeling drained by someone, this is a sure sign that the relationship has become toxic and a separation is called for. This may not be easy to do, but it is worth it and necessary for you to keep your peace and sanity. Surround yourself with faith builders and not faith killers, people that want to see you win. Some people just want to be around you to use you and to pollute your spirit because they are miserable deep down inside and misery loves company. Toxic people pretend that they are for you, but the minute they see your potential and progress, they try to attack your confidence. They may even try to turn others against you to discourage you from being all that God has created you to be – in fear that you will surpass them. They are also too insecure to admit that they really admire you, and can use your help.

- *Choose people who lift you up.* ~ Michelle Obama
- *Walk away from anything or anyone who takes away from your joy. Life is too short to put up with fools.* ~ Anonymous
- *Therefore, come out from them and be separate...* ~ 2 Corinthians 6:17
- *Surround yourself only with people who are going to take you higher.* ~ Oprah
- *What you can walk away from, you have mastered. What you can't walk away from has mastered you. He who loves the least controls the relationship. God is love.* ~ Rev Run

Tip #3: **Challenge your negative thoughts**

Your parents may not have told you how beautiful you are, or perhaps your spouse criticizes how you look after bearing children and compares you to other women, and your confidence may be on zero right now although you seem to look like you are okay around others. You may be feeling like giving up on yourself and feel unattractive behind the makeup, and the stylish clothes you wear. But don't give up! Be confident in the Lord. You were made in the image of God, and God says you are fearfully and wonderfully made. It is your time to shine! Therefore, you need to replace those negative thoughts with positive ones.

- *Your mind is a powerful thing. When you fill it with positive thoughts, your life will start to change.* ~ Anonymous
- *For as he thinks in his heart, so is he…* ~ Proverbs 23:7
- *Think positive and positive things will happen.* ~ Anonymous
- *Death and life are in the power of the tongue…* ~ Proverbs 18:21
- *Speak Life. Declare over your life daily:*
    I am Courageous, I am Unstoppable, I am Victorious, I am Love.
    I am Blessed, I am Gifted, I am Anointed, I am Successful.
    I am Healed, I am Healthy, I am Beautiful.
    I am Whole, I am Confident.
    I am Forgiving, I am Grateful, I am Generous.
    I am Strong, I am Favored, I am Able, I am Powerful, I am Fruitful.
    I am God's Masterpiece.
    ~ Anonymous

Tip #4: **Turn that frown upside down** ☺

If I say I will forget my complaint, I will change my expression, and smile. ~ Job 9:27

Studies show that: "One of the easiest and cheapest ways to boost your health, your mood, your longevity, and even your success is to smile. Smiles do a lot more than simply let the world know you are happy. They don't even have to be genuine to have some effect, but truest smiles do you the most good." The fact that you awoke this morning is a reason to smile.

- *Welcome today with a smile. It's God's gift to you!* ~ Anonymous
- *SMILE it will either warm their heart or piss them off, either*

way you win! ~ Anonymous
- *The longer your 'gevity is, the more confidence you build* ~ Kanye West

Tip #5: **Create a vision board**

Meditate and imagine the rewards you want your confidence to bring you, and write it down. Then create a vision board to bring your words to life. It provides you with incentive. It's also a great tool that can help you visualize the goals you want to achieve and motivate you to achieve them. Keep this vision board in a place where you can see it daily.
- *Write the vision; make it plain...* ~ Habakkuk 2:2
- *Do not throw away your confidence, it will be richly rewarded.* ~ Hebrews 10:35
- *Where there is no vision, the people perish.* ~ Proverbs 29:18
- *Create the highest, grandest vision possible for your life, because you become what you believe.* ~ Oprah Winfrey

Tip #6: **Eat a balanced diet**

If you throw away the junk food from your fridge and pantry, and replace them with foods with protein, fruits, and vegetables, and eat less sweets, carbs and fatty foods, you will feel much better and more energized because they are filled with a lot of minerals and vitamins that all help your body work better. Also, working out without having a balanced diet will not give you the best results as it would with a balanced diet. A balanced diet will even lessen your chance of fainting, getting sickness and diseases. Eating a balanced diet ought to be a lifestyle.
- *Make it a lifestyle, not a duty.* ~ Anonymous
- *Eat to Nourish Your Body.* ~ Anonymous
- *NOW IS THE Time to start treating your body like the temple that it is.* ~ Anonymous
- *You don't have to eat less, you just have to eat right.* ~ Anonymous
- *Let it be calorie-free, Jesus. Amen.* ~ Phaedra Parks

Tip #7: **Exercise Regularly**

Many people make excuses of why they won't exercise, like. . . "I just don't have the time," or say "I'm happy the way that I am," as if exercising indicates that you have low self-confidence or they think that exercising is vain. However, exercising is healthy and needs to be included in everyone's schedule. You will make time for what's important to you, and confident people take pride in their health through eating a balance diet and fitness. Studies show that physical activity controls your weight, reduce risk of cardiovascular disease, reduce the risk of diabetes, reduce the risk of cancer, strengthens your bones and muscles, improve your mental health, improve your ability to do daily activities and prevent fall, if you're an older adult and increase your chance of living longer.

- *Taking care of your body, no matter what your age, is an investment.* ~ Oprah Winfrey
- *If you have time for Facebook, you have time to exercise.* ~ Anonymous
- *I love my butter pecan ice cream, but I also love to workout. We all have our issues. Mine is arms and legs, keeping them tight and toned. It takes work, believe me.* ~ Beyoncé
- *EXERCISE -- TO Be FIT, NOT SKINNY EAT -- TO NOURISH YOUR BODY AND ALWAYS... IGNORE the HATERS, DOUBTERS and UNHEALTHY EXAMPLES that were once FEEDING YOU. – YOU ARE worth MORE than YOU realize.* ~ Anonymous
- *IF YOU'RE TOO BUSY TO WORK OUT, THEN YOUR PRIORITIES NEED TO CHANGE, I CAN'T THINK OF TOO MANY THINGS MORE IMPORTANT THAN YOUR HEALTH.* ~ Rolsey

Tip #8: **Set attainable goals**

It's great to dream big, but setting small attainable goals you can achieve in enough time will uplift you. Setting unrealistic big goals can feel overwhelming and frustrate you to the point that you give up trying to achieve it.

Studies show that one way you are more likely to achieve a goal is to use a technique called SMART:

- ◆ **S**pecific -- Be as precise as possible. Instead of "exercise," your goal should be something like "exercise 30 minutes per day.
- ◆ **M**easurable -- Come up with a way to measure your success. "Play guitar better" isn't measurable; "learn how to play one new song per week" is.
- ◆ **A**ttainable -- If there's no way you can reach your goal, you're setting yourself up for failure. "Save $100 a month" isn't attainable if you only have $50 left in your checking account after paying your bills.
- ◆ **R**ealistic -- Your goal should stretch you, but not necessarily be easy. "Never drink coffee again" may be less realistic than "only drink coffee once a week."
- ◆ **T**imely -- Set a clear time frame in which you want to reach your goal. If you don't have a deadline, you may not feel motivated to push yourself."-Anonymous

- *Setting goals is the first step in turning the invisible to the visible.* ~ Tony Robbins
- *Faith without works is DEAD.* ~ James 2:17"
- *The trouble with not having a goal is you can spend your life running up and down the field and never scoring.* ~ Rev Run

Tip #9: **Wear Confidence**

You can buy a $20 outfit and make it look like a million bucks on you if you wear it with confidence – wear clothes that suit your lifestyle and flatter you. If you can't afford high-end fashion that's ok, you don't have to keep up with the Kardashians. Shop at department stores that fit your budget. Be confident in knowing that you make the clothes, don't let the clothes make you.

- *The most beautiful thing a woman can wear is CONFIDENCE.* ~ Anonymous
- *The best accessory you can own is confidence.* ~ Anonymous
- *You'd be surprised at the things that look great on the outside but are dysfunctional on the inside. Be sure to function as good as you look.* ~ T.D. Jakes

Tip #10: **Groom yourself**

Take time to brush your teeth, gargle with mouth wash, wash your face, Shower, shave, wash your hair, blow dry and flat iron it, lotion your body, put on some chapstick, give yourself a pedicure and manicure, put on clean underwear, clean clothes, look polished. When you take time to care for yourself you will feel better about yourself, and it gives you the confidence you need to uplift others.

- *You have to take care of yourself, your body, your mind. Take care of your soul - be your own keeper.* ~ Jennifer Lopez
- *Don't lose yourself trying to be everything to everyone.* ~ Tony Gaskins
- *Taking care of yourself is part of taking care of your kids.* ~ Café Mom

Tip #11: **Stop comparing yourself to others**

Give yourself permission to run your own race. If you want to lose weight or tone your body, but you haven't worked out in a long time you don't need to start back up again with a vigorous workout just to prove something to someone, you want to start off small and work your way up to your ideal weight or cuts.

- *Comparison is the thief of Joy.* ~ Teddy Roosevelt
- *Happiness is found when you stop comparing yourself to other people.* ~ Anonymous
- *When you realize your true power...your true beauty those*

illusions of other people being better than you will begin to fade away. ~ beautyiswithin
- *You are fearfully and wonderfully made.* ~ Psalm 139:14

Tip #12: **Stay Connected**

Going to Summits and Conferences that have a relevant word to boost your confidence will refresh you every time. Stay refreshed.

- *Never stop embracing confidence.* ~ Darice Jordan
- *...do not throw away your confidence it will be richly rewarded.* ~ Hebrews 10:35
- *But blessed is the one who trusts in the LORD, whose confidence is in him.* ~ Jeremiah 17:7
- *Follow me as I follow Christ.* ~ Anonymous

<u>CONCLUSION</u>

Style is not all about wearing the latest trends. . .

STYLE IS CONFIDENCE ~ Darice Jordan

About Darice

I am Darice Jordan, from Queens, New York, born August 6, 1980, a proud parent of three (Diamond, August and Darren), a Christian for 13 years now, and a work-in-progress. I am currently a Fivefold Ministry participant for almost a year now in the Fivefold Ministry Leadership program taught by my Pastor, Dr. Riva Tims, at our church, Majestic Life Ministries, where I am being equipped and trained to properly operate in the Fivefold Ministry, and I may be ordained upon the completion of this program in June of 2017. Today, I am a Confidence Life Coach. I love uplifting others. I am also the proud owner of a new business, "King and Queen Posh Lifestyle, LLC" that will provide Confidence Coaching Summits on a quarterly basis. These summits are designed to inspire and empower you to be the best you can be – inside and out. My Confidence Coaching stems from a biblical and spiritual perspective. At the age of 17, I gave birth to my first child, my daughter Diamond; at the age of 18, I graduated high school with a Diploma and married the father of my child (who was nineteen and imprisoned at the time).

I'm sure you can imagine our struggles with me being a young, single parent and prisoner's wife trying to survive on the streets, and him being a young black man trying to survive behind the walls of prison for 16 years. Living under these circumstances wasn't always easy for us, it was heart breaking. I wasn't always as confident as I am today. In the early years, being a prisoner's wife, I felt depressed. I lacked self-confidence and had a poor image of myself, so I would look for love in all the wrong places – in smoking, drinking and in toxic relationships. Like the Samaritan woman at the well (see: John Chapter 4), I was thirsty for the void inside me to be filled. In 2006, I rededicated my life to the Lord and ever since then, I have been going from glory to glory. To God be the glory.

I also cannot forget witnessing what other prisoner's spouses and families had to endure on my trips Up North. I remember one of the wives confessing to me how depressed she was, after leaving her husband from a trailer visit they had together, and how it left her feeling so very depressed that she had to be admitted to the hospital for a week after this. Well, because of what I have been through, I have learned a lot. I can see that there are other women who struggle like I did.

My mission is to help them, and to help them take control of their life again.

Notes:
To stay connected, updated and encouraged, follow Darice on Instagram:
  • @darice_jordan
And be on the lookout for Darice's first RED CARPET CONFIDENCE SUMMIT:
  • #STYLEISCONFIDENCE

CHAPTER 13

ROCK BOTTOM TO E-COMMERCE ROCK STAR
SEVEN STRATEGIES TO CREATING AND SUSTAINING SUCCESS

BY SAM E. COHEN

In October of 2010, I hit rock bottom. It's an expression I'd heard often but never truly understood... until I sat in a jail cell for five days. At that point, there was no doubt in my mind I was experiencing rock bottom and it was intensely more miserable than those two words could ever communicate. I was a high-level executive earning six figures at an electronics manufacturer in New York City. When the economy shifted in 2008, we received word there would be massive layoffs and pay cuts.

With the writing on the wall, I ventured out on my own. During 2009 and 2010, I did whatever it took to pay the bills. My personal life in shambles from a prior divorce added to the difficulties. Child support payments became impossible to keep up with, which subsequently resulted in a five-day jail sentence. It was indeed my darkest hour; my children were without my support and without me. If you're a parent, you will understand.

Instead of wondering, "How did I get here?" I made a promise to myself and to my children, to never end up there again. Hitting rock bottom once, was enough for me. I decided to **take charge of my life** and make something of myself, by becoming self-employed.

For most of my life I chased money, always moving from one job to another to earn the next highest salary. I realized I needed to take control and start attracting money instead of chasing it; which is an important distinction. Instead of following the money, I decided to take massive action to make myself more valuable and therefore attract more money.

In the beginning stages of 2009, I began doing everything I could to earn a living and I started selling DVDs at local flea markets. I had previous success with eBay, so I decided to get back into the e-commerce market by attempting to sell 1,000 DVDs for $1,000. An interested buyer contacted me about the quality of the DVDs. He asked how many were superb quality and I answered honestly, "about 50". He still seemed interested so I asked what he planned to do with the DVDs. He explained he had a business as a third-party seller on Amazon. I had no idea this even existed.

I instantly realized this was my opportunity to earn a living on my own terms, to become my own boss, and to **take charge of my life.** I jumped headfirst into becoming a third-party Amazon seller. At the time, there was little to no information on how to sell on Amazon. I had no idea what I was doing, but I knew to succeed I had to **keep learning**. The first six months were grueling, to say the least. I was not the most tech-savvy guy, but once I figured out Amazon's rules, things became easier.

The process of buying and selling came naturally to me through work experience and lessons my father taught me. He owned stores in Newark, New Jersey and he knew how to seize opportunities he was presented with. When I was 12 years old, my father's stores sold basic dry goods throughout the year, but strategically added toys during the holiday season. At that time, Cabbage Patch dolls were the hottest Christmas item. My father called his supplier and when he found out they were sold out until January, he opened the cash register, took out $2,000 and he, my mother, my siblings and I went to every Toys "R" Us in New York and New Jersey and bought every Cabbage Patch doll. We paid $60 each and sold them for $200. It was a great Christmas for everyone and a lesson I never forgot.

My father not only taught me how to buy, sell and negotiate, but he had a zest for life that I aspire to emulate each day. This perhaps was his most valued gift to me. My father passed away at the young age of 49, when I was only 19, but he lived his life with zeal and passion that rivaled men twice his age. When times were tough during my first six months selling on Amazon, I often recalled the example my father set of never giving up; and in that time, I went from selling DVDs for $1 each at flea markets to making $100,000 in monthly sales. Now, in my sixth year selling, I am doing $20,000,000 in sales a year.

Today, my Amazon business is in the top one percent of third party sellers, out of more than 2 million sellers. This is proof that you don't need a lot of money or experience to be successful in this business. One very important thing I did to create success was to *surround myself with quality people.* At the time there were no teachers, mentors, or consultants to show you how to start, let alone succeed as a third-party seller. I figured it out on my own through tens of thousands of hours of trial and error, but quickly realized I needed a strong network to become effective. I started by recruiting my amazing wife, whom I married in June of 2011. She had a steady, high paying job utilizing her Master's Degree in Social Work, but it was important for me to have her by my side. She agreed to leave her job and – work alongside me.

Once my wife was on board things began to really take off. When we first started, we were working out of our one bedroom apartment selling DVDs. We didn't even have space to organize the DVDs, so every sale was a treasure hunt. I quickly realized we needed a bigger and improved working space. I went directly to the office landlord and explained my dire need for space, but I only had limited funds with a lack of credit and no references. Luckily, the landlord was one of those quality people who had faith in me. He showed me a commercial leasing opportunity and as I looked around I noticed it included the exact printer that I needed, but couldn't afford, which matched the specific needs of an e-commerce business. The landlord agreed to throw it in with the lease.

I took the deal and signed a lease for the 600-square foot space, including the printer. Today, we operate out of a 16,000-square foot warehouse and office space, complete with forklifts, pallet racks, and loading docks. We employ close to 30 people, including performance coaches, product and sales experts, administration staff and warehouse staff. To quote author, life coach and speaker Tony Robbins, "The defining factor is never resources; it's resourcefulness."

To grow a business housed in my one bedroom apartment to one in a 16,000-square foot facility, it took a lot of hard work as well as a lot of innovative ideas. I learned to think outside the box. One of our many sourcing strategies is retail arbitrage. One example of our efficacious retail arbitrage took place when Walmart announced it was closing a few stores. As soon as I heard this I sought the closest store closing near me – nearly 3 hours away in Baltimore - and sent three employees and a truck to the store. They purchased $35,000 of merchandise on clearance. It took them six hours to check out! We were then able to sell the merchandise at retail prices and grossed well over $100,000 in sales. The story was featured in the *Wall Street Journal*.

This is one example of how we find the best ways to source

products to meet consumer and Amazon demands, whether it is direct from manufacturers, retailers, or even through manufacturing our own products. Amazon relies on third party sellers to supply products they cannot obtain and we are dedicated to meeting those demands through innovative thinking.

On the road to success, I learned to **value time**. When we first began, we were managing all processes of our business. Now, we utilize Amazon fulfillment services instead. In place of packing, shipping, handling returns and other customer service issues, we outsource them to Amazon. We simply ship our products to Amazon, which allows customers to buy our products through Amazon Prime and thus utilize Amazon's low shipping rates, expert management, and superb customer service. By making smart time management use, we can focus on our core business and free our time for greater revenue-generating work.

Over the next few years our business continued to grow in size and success. We doubled in size every year and our profit margins increased year over year. In October 2014, I was invited to spend two days at the Amazon headquarters, as a member of the top 1% of Amazon third party sellers, to provide feedback and suggestions to other seller support staff. I was indeed, honored to be chosen. This business is a great opportunity, but can also be difficult to figure out without proper guidance. This is one reason why I seek opportunities to help others find their own success. I am a strong believer in the **abundance mentality**. There is plenty of success to go around for anyone who is willing to work hard. I believe those who have achieved success should support others on the path.

By January 2015, I realized I was spending a substantial amount of time answering questions about becoming a successful third party Amazon seller. I truly loved doing it, but realized it was consuming a disproportionate amount of my time. I built a trustworthy reputation as an expert on e-commerce and Amazon, and I was writing and speaking on many platforms. In April

2015, we began to develop our consulting program and officially launched it in July 2015. The plan was to work with a small group of sellers to teach them the secrets to making money selling on Amazon. We would serve as their consulting experts. People thought I was crazy, that I would cannibalize my own business, but my belief in the abundance mentality held strong.

We decided to offer our consulting services to a limited group of 100 people over the course of a year as a Platinum Annual Membership for $5,000. Amazon Consulting Experts, as we named it, officially launched with its first group of clients in July of 2015, teaching all the intricacies and nuances of being an Amazon third party seller, along with business, life, and personal development skills. We shared best practices with our consulting clients on how to interact with Amazon customers, employees, vendors, attorneys, accountants and other stakeholders. The results were amazing.

Amazon is a constantly evolving marketplace, so being an active seller is a huge asset in helping our clients. We are in the trenches alongside them. The ability to share the challenges our Amazon business faces, and solutions we find, goes a long way with our clients and their results.

One of our motivating factors is seeing our client's successes. I remember when I first met Michael. He was a man in his 50s who had recently lost his home to foreclosure. He had to borrow money for the program and inventory and now he is making over two million dollars a year in gross sales on Amazon and earning about $400,000 to $500,000 a year in net profit! Another client, Scott, is a pharmaceutical rep with a great job making six figures a year. He is also a very talented musician. His dream is to run his Amazon business and have time to play his music. He is steadily working towards leaving his corporate job and pursuing his dream. I am determined to help him, and others like him, to provide the opportunity to run a business they can fit around their lifestyle.

My first group of consulting clients had a 98% success rate and 95% signed up for a second year. Amazon is a dynamic marketplace, and our clients benefit from our team experience and evolution within our own business. The right support can truly make your business a success. They learned, just as I did, that surrounding yourself with quality people is a key to success.

Amazon Consulting Experts is a way for people to realize the dream I realized, and to live with passion. It provides us an opportunity to share our success with others. My Amazon business sustains me while my consulting business fulfills me. I now jump out of bed at 5:00am every morning excited to start my day. There hasn't been a day in almost six years, since I started my business, when I wasn't excited to go to work. I never miss any of my family's events. I AM MY OWN BOSS AND LIVE BY MY OWN DECISIONS.

You too, can experience the same freedom and success in your own life. Just remember several key mentalities that helped me make it to where I am today, a successful business owner with 30 employees doing $20 million dollars in sales a year and helping hundreds of people find success in their own lives. This is possible because I took charge of my life, committed to always learning, never gave up, surrounded myself with quality people, welcomed innovative thinking, valued my time, and committed to the abundance mentality.

I think of these actions as my Seven Strategies to Create Sustaining and Fulfilling Success:

1. Take Charge of Your Life – Take 100% responsibility for all aspects of your life
2. Always Keep Learning – Be naturally curious and willing to learn
3. Never Give Up – Sometimes you have to take two steps forward and one step back

4. Surround Yourself with Quality People – Others have a huge impact on your life
5. Welcome Innovative Thinking – "Break the mold" and do things differently than everyone else
6. Value Your Time – Stop trading time for money
7. Commit to the Abundance Mentality – There are always chances and opportunities available to all

This is not the end of my story. Just as I serve as a consultant and mentor to others, I continue to seek mentorship myself. These Seven Strategies are a roadmap to success and are vital to achievement. They have been the driving force behind my success. Once you achieve your level of success, you'll find it's not about the money you've made, but about the person you become in the process. All that I have achieved is nowhere near as gratifying as the ability to have positively impacted and changed lives. It's my mission to help as many people as possible transition to the future – which is e-commerce – and more importantly, to help them build their dream life around their successes. Remember these Seven Strategies and you too will uncover success waiting for you.

About Sam

Sam E. Cohen currently resides in New Jersey with his wife and four children and has been in e-commerce for 20 years. He started selling on Amazon in 2011, and founded Amazon Consulting Experts (ACE) in 2015. In that time, Sam's business has become one of the top 1% of all third-party sellers on Amazon. He employs 30 people, and owns and operates multiple Amazon accounts with express written permission from Amazon. Sam has been an invited guest at Amazon headquarters in Seattle to discuss current and future business goals and concerns, and was featured on National Public Radio's *Planet Money* and in *The Wall Street Journal.*

Sam is very passionate about mentoring, consulting, teaching, motivating and inspiring other business people. He has been helping other Amazon sellers for the past five years, both as a consultant for large businesses as well as entrepreneurial individuals just starting out and looking to get on board. From this experience, Amazon Consulting Experts (ACE) was born – an exclusive, custom-tailored consulting, mentoring and training program.

Sam believes in paying it forward by teaching people "how to fish" and the abundance mentality. Sam strives to find a balance in life and has a supportive family behind him. Sam also believes in employing as many people as possible given the sluggish economy, and routinely helps people who are financially struggling. For the past 25 years, Sam has worked closely with a charity for terminally-ill children all over the world and a portion of what he earns goes to this amazing charity.

If you would like additional information on how the ACE program helps new entrepreneurs get started – or how it can help grow an existing business – by effectively utilizing e-commerce tools, retail arbitrage and Amazon third-party selling techniques, your inquiries are welcome via their web site.

Sam is available for speaking engagements and media interviews.

Contact Sam via his website or call:
• Web Site: www.amazonconsultingexperts.com
• Phone: (732) 695-6355

CHAPTER 14

SIMPLE WAYS TO GUARANTEE YOU WILL NEVER RUN OUT OF MONEY

BY SCOTT ZIMMERMAN

Having been in the financial services industry for almost 30 years, I have come to realize that most people that are nearing retirement, and some that have already retired, haven't planned sufficiently for themselves, their spouses, children and grandchildren. Most people tell me that they wish they would have planned better, and taken the extra time to ensure they had the proper coverage. Many people seem to live for today and put off the planning that is so essential. What is really interesting is that if younger people simply get in the game, and implement a plan early on, it is far easier to plan for their future. And, since it is reasonable to believe that we can be in retirement for as long, if not longer than the length of years we actually work, it is even more critical to address this issue. Achieving true financial freedom and peace of mind during retirement is definitely attainable!

This subject is near and dear to my heart!

"My parents did not do the proper planning during their lifetime. My mother was a saver, my father a spender. That combination did not work well for them financially."

My entire childhood, I grew up hearing how financially strapped they were – struggling to pay the bills, not getting ahead, and never feeling at ease that their future was secure. Thankfully, my mother (the planner) had the foresight to obtain a small amount of life insurance, as well as Long Term Care insurance, on my father. I am grateful every day for my mother's vision. My father recently passed away, and these end-of-life provisions provided my mother, and the entire family, with a great sense of comfort. His long-term care insurance made it feasible for him to receive the proper care, and live out his days in a dignified way. And, it saved her from depleting her savings. <u>This small amount of life insurance also made an enormous impact on her ability to survive without him here.</u> I miss my father. We all loved him. His health issues, however, had they persisted into his 80's or 90's, would have had an extremely detrimental impact on their lives, and caused serious financial hardship.

My goal is to help as many people as possible plan sufficiently for their future, so they can live in retirement exactly the way they envision – providing protection for themselves and the ones they love, and creating guarantees that they never, ever run out of money.

I consult with my clients to advise and assist them with mapping out their retirement years, and what will be necessary in order for them to live the lifestyle they dream about. I bring many issues to the forefront, so no stone is left unturned – protection in the event of illness, protection for their spouses in the event of an early disability or untimely death, and protection to ensure they don't outlive their savings.

THE PROBLEM...

Most people are not aware of what they have or what they should be doing. They partake in their company retirement plans, investing in strategies that may not necessarily lead them to accomplishing their financial goals. They just put their future on auto-cruise and hope for the best.

Most people have access to social security, but there is concern about the future solvency of the social security system. Today, the vast majority of companies do not offer pension plans. At one time, they were the norm, and you could rest easy knowing you were taken care of in retirement. Now, it's up to you to put your money to work efficiently to secure your future.

It's hard to know what to do or who to trust when you're bombarded with information from TV personalities, banking institutions, and financial advisors who may not be taking the best interest of the client into account. As a result, people get confused about how to move forward. Often times, people fail to take any action at all, which only compounds the problem.

Another huge dilemma is that people are living longer than ever before. It used to be a big deal when Willard Scott announced on the Today Show that someone reached the age of 100. Life expectancy for a man today is 78, and for a woman, 81. With the advancement of medical technology, life expectancy will increase. No one knows who will be lucky enough to live into their 90's or 100's, which is why it is even more critical for people to plan for their future.

So, you ask...*WHAT IS THE SOLUTION TO THESE PROBLEMS?*

I'm an expert in this particular area, and have worked with thousands of people to structure solid retirement plans. When planning, there is a lot to take into consideration to make sure you end up where you want to be. And, I always recommend that my clients consult with their CPA or Estate Planning Attorney to obtain the appropriate tax and legal advice.

If you're getting ready to retire or you are already retired, I recommend considering safe money investments. If you are currently drawing from your retirement funds, or getting close to doing so, and your money is in the market, now is the time to protect it in the event of a correction. For those who have done well, saved enough, and have accumulated enough to retire, it is an excellent time to move some of this money into safe investments. So many people at this stage of their life have too much of their savings and investments at risk. If the market drops as it did in 2008, and you were to lose 20%, 30% or even 40%, could you handle this type of financial loss? And, could you ride it out and wait for the market to recover? If you continue to draw from these investments while the market is down, you are bound to drain your accounts, leaving you and your loved ones exposed to a potentially harmful financial situation. Would you elect to have your children, or other family members, pay your living expenses because you didn't plan accordingly?

1. THERE ARE MANY SAFE MONEY INVESTMENTS

These are investments that have only upside potential, with no downside risk. You can invest in the market, without the risk normally associated with it. If the market has a down year, you get zero return, but if the market is enjoying an upswing, you get a large piece of the gain. You can't lose a penny!

When I meet with people, and I see they have a substantial amount invested in stocks, mutual funds, 401(k), etc., and they are getting close to retirement, I will usually recommend that they only risk what they can afford to lose. If they have time to recover from any significant loss in the market, they can ride it out, but I advise my clients to take the part of their investments that they cannot afford to lose, and put that into a safe investment. Only gamble with the amount they can afford to lose. Some people think the market will continue to rise. The last decade has been great, but if you follow the market, history shows it will correct again. It's going to happen… If you've done well in the past 9-10 years, it may be time to take some of your winnings off the table, and place it somewhere safe, where you can still get nice returns on your investments.

I ask my clients, and any prospective clients, "Would you prefer a sure thing or a maybe?"

Most people that are nearing retirement or are retired usually say, a sure thing. It makes sense!

There are some great investments that are not only guaranteed, but also guarantee an ongoing stream of income. Income for the rest of your life, guaranteed! If you have a spouse, and you were to pass away, your spouse would get the same exact income for the rest of their life, guaranteed. If any of your investment is left, it would be a passed down to your loved ones.

When it comes to retirement income, most people are seeking peace of mind, and not a life where they are worrying about watching the stock market daily, or worrying about potentially devastating events affecting the economy, or waking up at 2:00 a.m. worrying if they will be financially protected. Overall, it's important to understand all the pieces of the puzzle.

2. LONG TERM CARE (LTC)

Let's face facts. *Statistically, 70% of people over the age of 65 will need some form of long term care for an extended period of time.* That's 7 out of 10 people. These statistics are real! Statistically, people need 4.5 years of care in their home (Home Health Coverage) and 2.5 years in a nursing home (Nursing Home Coverage). Of course, individual needs will vary – some will require this type of care for shorter time periods, and others, longer. I have helped many people put this type of planning in place, and I always tell them, I hope this is the biggest waste of money ever and you never need to collect on this. But, the fact is, we don't know how the end of our lives will play out.

Who needs LTC? If you have a spouse you want to protect if you become ill, or if you would like to be able to choose for yourself who takes care of you and where you will receive that care, or if you have assets you wish to protect, this may be the best money you ever spend.

LTC coverage can be very reasonably priced. There are many different types of plans in the marketplace, so the consumer has choices. Before I delve into a few of these plans, I would like you to imagine the following:

If you were a single 60, 70, 80, or 90-year-old, who would take care of you if you needed care? Your kids? Your friends? Would you really want your kids to have to change and clean you, and take care of you in this way? And, do you think they would want to have to do this? Of course, they would be there for you, but it's a very difficult, and sometimes traumatic, experience to endure. And, if you were 60, 70, 80 or 90 years old and you had a spouse or significant other, would you want them to have to care for you in this way - clean you, change you, etc.? Imagine if you fall down. Could your spouse pick you up? These are difficult questions. From personal experience, I saw my mother struggling to help my father out of the bathtub. At this point, they made the decision to call in additional care, as it was just too much for her to handle.

When buying LTC coverage, your advisor will research the going rates in your area. Generally, you will buy a daily or monthly benefit amount, and you receive that amount for a pre-determined period of time, should you ever need it. So, you choose how long you would want your policy to pay for your care - 3, 4, 5, or 6 years, are the most common choices. There is usually a waiting period, called an elimination period - 30, 60, 90, or 180 days. During this elimination period, you would pay for your care in the event you needed it, and after that point, your LTC Plan would kick in and begin paying for services. There are some other options - Inflation protection options. You could add this feature to keep up with LTC inflation costs. The cost of care is rising every year, so I would recommend adding this type of protection. There are still a few companies that offer unlimited care, as well.

There are also several types of plans that you can choose from:

"Regular Long Term Care." This insurance is traditional coverage. This is pay-as-you-go, for the rest of your life. If you need care, most companies have a 90-day period where you can stop making payments after having 90 days of care.

"Life with LTC coverage." With this, you can buy a life insurance policy, and tap into the death benefit for your LTC needs, if necessary. If you pass away, having never used any of the Long Term Care benefits, your death benefit remains as is.

"Hybrid plans." There are a few different plans, but here is an example of one: you can put $100,000 into the plan, and it will remain fully liquid. At any time, the $100,000 can be taken out. If you pass away, there is a death benefit, and if you need it for long term care needs, those funds will be there for you. You can't lose! Cash is yours at any time, and if you pass away, your beneficiary receive a nice tax free benefit.

3. LIFE INSURANCE

Life insurance is very important, as it is the ultimate protection for your loved ones. Planning correctly will help your spouse so that if something happens to you, they would be taken care of financially. Many people obtain life insurance for legacy planning purposes. You can have it structured where it benefits your children and grandchildren, for generations to come. These funds can be paid out each year, to provide lasting financial relief. You can also specify your favorite charity as a beneficiary. You will certainly never be forgotten!

Life insurance is the least expensive way to pay for estate taxes. If your net worth is high enough, estate taxes will be due within nine months after you pass. Right now, estate taxes are at about 40%. So, if you had a high estate value and you pass away, 40% of your estate value could be taxed and again, due in nine months. With Life Insurance in place, the cost is pennies on the dollar!

Life insurance could be used to pay off debt so that you wouldn't leave your family high and dry, wondering how they will pay the bills. It can be utilized as a replacement of income. If you were earning $50,000 and you had a $1,000,000 life insurance policy, given the funds from the life insurance policy were invested and earning 5%, it could easily replace your income.

I could go on and on why people need or could use a solid life insurance plan. When it comes down to it, you buy life insurance to take care of your loved ones and the people you care about most.

In fact, the subjects that we have been talking about are all about Love. Loving yourself, your family, and others. I wish I had more space to give you all the information you need, but I hope this helps to get you started in preparing to care for the people that are most important to you!

About Scott

Scott Zimmerman helps his clients strategize properly for their financial future, to ensure they have fail-safe planning in place to maximize their peace of mind. He makes certain that their investments are in the right products, so they're never ever exposed to the risk of running out of money. Scott establishes a secure plan in which his clients have the ultimate protection and coverage necessary for themselves, their spouses, and their loved ones.

Helping clients achieve "peace of mind" is Scott's goal. He listens carefully to their needs, and customizes a plan that is structured exactly the way they want it. People have a lot of choices when it comes to their coverage. Scott knows it's not a one-size-fits-all type of industry, so he goes above and beyond to identify his clients' objectives, so that they reach their desired target.

Scott has been a trusted advisor, speaker, and author within the financial services industry since 1989, and is a Partner of a financial services firm in Los Angeles, California. In addition, he is the co-creator of the Life Insurance Audit, The Annuity Audit, The 21st Century HR Solution, and the Perfect LTC Solution.

His true passion in life is his family, which includes his two daughters, Samantha and Taylor, his better half Debbie, and her children - Sydney, Gabby, Izzy and Niko. Scott enjoys traveling, golf, working out, skiing and spending quality time with family and friends.

You can connect with Scott at:
- Scott@Corpstrat.com
- www.Corpstrat.com
- www.SafeMoneyScott.com
- www.SafeMoneyScott.com/blog/
- www.linkedin.com/in/scott-zimmerman-9463a12/
- www.howtherichgetricher.com
- www.twitter.com/Scottyzim
- www.facebook.com/scott.zimmerman.75491

CHAPTER 15

THE BROKEN MILLIONAIRE
MY JOURNEY TO SPIRITUAL AND FINANCIAL WEALTH

BY DEMETRIUS EARLY

You can have the money and the lifestyle, but what remains if it's taken away matters most.

Have you ever had a moment of reckoning? If you have, you know those are tough situations. They're often embarrassing, debilitating, and humbling. My "moment of reckoning" came when I was face-to-face with my manmade maker—the judge— as I tried to explain my position.

I'd been fortunate to find a career that I loved in real estate. The money was more than good; it was great. My life was filled with adventure and opportunity. By all appearances and accounts, I'd arrived—and I was young enough to enjoy it. I was invincible! I had the world and all its potential in my hands. I was in control of the wheel. Then came the sharp turn that drove me right off the road and down into a valley. I was truly dumbfounded by it.

The roots of our life's issues are found under the weeds
that cover our emotional garden.

That judge sentenced me to seventeen years, saying that it was more important to serve the time than reimburse the money that was at the root of my legal challenge. Sitting in prison, I had time to think about the man I was, and what I'd lost. The money was, strangely enough, secondary. I'd grown up really poor, living in Shreveport, LA, with my grandmother. My parents were not involved and it wasn't always easy to understand why. My grandmother had brought me home from the hospital and raised me. I was grateful for her love and I definitely knew that I didn't want to be like so many others around me. I would not be:

- Stuck in poverty
- The next statistic for a young black man's death (I'd known eighteen kids who died by the time I graduated high school)
- A non-involved parent when I decided to have children

My motivation to make something of myself started off early in life as a result. Nothing was going to be handed to me, or come easy, so I knew I had to be resourceful and figure out a way that would work, no matter how different it was.

After being involved in a shoot-out and receiving some kind words from an elderly neighbor lady, I was spurred to go live with my father. I didn't know him and when I first saw him I was shocked at how much we looked alike. Life there wasn't great, either, and we butted heads often enough, but I did have the chance to play football. That was good for me. Nothing thrilled me more than when I got the opportunity to play college football after high school. I could have cared less about grades, but I felt accomplished when I got to play ball. It was my golden ticket, I thought. After college, I got an agent and tried out for a few NFL teams, but it ended up not working out, because I blew the chance by getting into some trouble.

With football out of the picture, I needed a new plan and my future was looking pretty lousy. In one year, I had eleven W2s. I was shuffling through opportunities as fast as a Vegas dealer shuffles cards. While working in New York, visiting in the garment district, I went into a store that had amazing ties and a great idea came to me. Professionals needed to look good, and I could be the one to help them make it happen. I'd identified my target audience, and then got to work. I negotiated the price of the ties down, made an investment in them, and brought them back to Houston. My trunk was open for business—yes, I sold them out of my car's trunk. It took just one great $10K month to get me hooked on the money.

My ability to connect with others was a gift I decided to use to make my dreams become reality.

My football agent and I had remained in touch. When he heard what I was doing and saw how I could connect with people, he suggested I should go into real estate. I loved the idea, especially the promise of making more money. It was good fortune and I also felt an immediate passion for the business. The result was:

1. I committed all my financial assets.
2. I committed to a partnership with my agent in real estate investing.
3. I committed all my energy to earn money and experience success.

Then…my agent took it all, forcing me to take destiny by the hand. I couldn't let it stop me. I had big things to do.

My ego was a bit bruised, but my commitment was unwavering so I decided to start my own real estate investment company. A trusted friend asked if I wanted to partner in with him on a mortgage company, and I was stoked about the opportunity. We took off with a bang, and things were going so well! I was doing seminars and helping people fix their credit so they could live the American dream. Everything I touched seemed to produce results.

I moved to bolder visions and entered into the luxury home market, and I was "wowed" by the explosive growth of that market and how it changed my life. It seemed that God was blessing me ten-fold for the rougher moments in my past. I was a young millionaire with the charisma and a business card to prove my worth. It came with a price, though, because my personal life grew rocky, creating challenges with my wife and kids. But my professional life—totally smooth. It was my priority.

Then came my "ego deflate-gate". I'd been getting audited more and more, and to me it was a sign of my success. I was quite young to have as much wealth as I did. It turned out, I was actually being investigated and soon enough, one big mistake took me down faster than I'd risen.

A New and Needed Perspective

Every decision I'd made in my adult life was focused on "why."
I'd paid little attention to "who" I was meant to be.

Each day during the low point of my life, I found myself reflecting on the importance of the things I once had undervalued. I missed my kids badly and my marriage had crumbled. Now those things were important to me. This low point surprisingly became my saving grace, as it allowed me to find God. I was forced to reconcile my past—the pain, the poverty, the ego, the lack of accountability for my actions, and look past those things and to the future. God had a plan for me, and he'd guided me to that place and time to discover it.

The constant reminders of failure and destitution in my life circumstances would intuitively seem uninspiring, but the mental toughness and drive that God had given me from birth, and the new revelation of what was really important, was the only way forward and my pillar of strength. I became fully aware of what I should be doing. Nothing beats God-powered determination.

This spark was smoldering in me and my purpose was about to be set on fire.

With God and faith in my life, where I was physically located and being broke didn't matter as much. I didn't want to be in prison, of course, but by growing spiritually wealthy everything began to click. I knew what my gifts were—inspiring and helping others to achieve great things—but I'd never used them to serve my purpose through the lens of God's amazing eye. When I was released from prison after only nine years, I was ready to work. I knew that I'd have a lot to do, but I felt equipped for the challenge.

A New Beginning

Accept responsibility for your life. Know that it is you who will get you where you want to go, no one else.
~ Les Brown

My rebuilding of relationships with my family members commenced with my attending one of my son's birthday party. So much had been missed in his life, and it made me aware of the judgments we all make. What had taken place in my life had hurt my family and made me a "non-involved" parent. Go figure…

As fate would have it, I also received a call that my grandmother was sick and near death at that very same birthday party. This woman meant everything to me and I always knew she was a gift from God, but knowing she might be gone before she could see the man I'd grown into was so scary. I rushed back to Louisiana to see her, hoping for just one day. I was given fifty days. During that time, it was hard to watch her suffer, but it reaffirmed that God needed me to learn compassion, despite the heartbreaking challenges of the situation.

Nothing was more powerful to me during those days than when my grandmother looked at me and said, "Demetrius, stop apologizing and feeling guilty for your success. Don't worry about us. Find your own family and don't worry about how others feel. Focus on the good you can do." Those words meant so much to me, because when I made money, I gave it freely to my family, in hopes of improving their lives. My intentions were good, and I wanted to empower them to something greater, but all I did was enable them to keep asking and asking, never evaluating what they had to give. And when I lost the money, they were gone right along with it.

A short time later I met an amazing woman named Katrina. Without a doubt, she was God's gift to me for my new start. I met her one day and called her the next day to have coffee. We met and started with our largest concerns. She was a breast cancer survivor, and I was inspired by her courage. Not to mention her courage to look at me and not run after she found out I'd spent all that time in prison. As we opened our hearts, the connection was clear. When I put my hand on hers and experienced this intense, eternal goodness in her, I knew I'd fallen in love. I proposed that day, knowing that neither one of us wanted to take a day for granted. Four and a half months later, Katrina and I were married.

The Glory of Helping Others

With the right guidance, we can all solve and resolve our greatest challenges.

My passion for the real estate industry was legitimate, despite all the troubles it had cost me. As I thought about what came next for me, I recognized a few things that were certainties in my life:

- Being an entrepreneur was where I could do the most good.
- Investing in real estate was something that I truly enjoyed.
- Helping people with their credit counseling to recognize the dream of home ownership was powerful and inspiring.

I opened up a credit reform company called We Raise Your Credit Score, Inc. My hometown of Shreveport was the perfect place for this business, as Northwest Louisiana is the fourth worst area of the country for credit challenges. I wanted to give authentic help to credit-challenged customers, but what I found through this has truly opened up the gateway of what I believe to be God's intention for me.

Credit struggles are most often the symptom to an underlying problem. When that problem is addressed and someone can heal, the credit crisis they have will also heal.

My intention is to help as many people as possible live a better life on all levels, including financially. This has revealed emotional wealth and abundance that compel me to move forward every day. My success now is limitless because I made the decision to do the right thing. I'm a better person and businessman as a result. Katrina and I have also started Make Me, Mold Me Empowerment, Inc. as a way to help connect people who are trying to find their way to the prosperity that comes through living a life that honors both God and their fullest potential.

This is inspiration that is shared in seminars, as well as by my weekly visits to the prison system. I want to talk with young men and engage them into thinking about their fullest potential. These interactions help all of us to reveal amazing lessons and revelations in our lives.

Seven Lessons to Guide You Personally and Professionally

Finding our fulfillment is a great and worthwhile pursuit.

Whether a lesson is big or small, it can make a profound impact on your ability to honestly assess yourself and the environment you set yourself up in. You were born to thrive, but you have to participate in your results.

1. Look yourself in the eyes
   Be honest about who you are so you can experience authentic

growth that guides you toward your limitless potential.

2. **Understand God's purpose for your life**

   Take time to remember that God's purpose for your life never goes away, and His purpose is always good. Ask yourself: why abandon it?

3. **Forgiveness**

   Through forgiveness you open up the doors to move forward with good intentions and with balance in your heart and mind.

4. **Believe in yourself and be determined not to quit**

   It isn't always going to be easy, but if you are pursuing the right thing, every challenge you encounter is worth it. You will grow in ways greater than you can guess.

5. **Know your financial house**

   Where you put your money to work for you needs to be monitored by you. Take accountability for your results and outcomes.

6. **Write down your goals and business plans**

   Writing what we desire brings it to life and lays the seeds for growth. Your action is the fertilizer that will help it take hold in your life.

7. **Build a team that believes in your vision**

   We are not meant to do things alone. We need to have a spiritual team, a personal team, and a professional team that we are aligned with and that works in each other's best interests.

Be inspired by these lessons and their importance in your life. Apply them freely! Your God-given purpose is calling you, and it wants you to live your best life.

About Demetrius

The life of Demetrius Early is a true rags-to-riches story. Now a self-made millionaire, successful entrepreneur, speaker, author and mentor, he is passionate about helping people overcome their mental, and sometimes physical blocks. His desire is to take his experiences, his knowledge about finance, business development, personal motivation, success and much more, to the people. He wants to give people a second chance at achieving success in their lives, whatever that might mean.

When human beings experience trauma or severe life stressors, it is not uncommon for their lives to unravel. However, Demetrius Early has mastered the art of turning a negative situation into a positive one. Born into the poverty-stricken streets of the Mooretown neighborhood in Shreveport, Louisiana, Demetrius learned quickly that you must take responsibility for your life. He graduated from high school with a desire to become more than a product of his environment. He attended college, where he also had a successful football career, before making a decision that landed him behind bars.

Demetrius knew that a life of crime was not a life for him. He understood his purpose and vowed to make a difference the day he was destined for freedom. He did just that. Today, he is a loving husband to his wife Katrina, and together they have created a nonprofit organization, Make Me Mold Me Empowerment, Inc. Part of his role is mentoring young men – both free and imprisoned. He strives to unlock the physical bars of the correction facility as well and the mental bars of their minds that may be keeping them from reaching their full potential.

In his endeavor to help more people, Demetrius is also the founder and CEO of We Raise Your Credit Score Inc., which does more than just help people repair their credit score. Demetrius works closely with his clients to help them change their mindset and achieve success they never thought imaginable– such as buying their own homes, starting their own businesses, etc.

Demetrius has started and built several successful businesses, but has never forgotten where he came from. His story is one of inspiration for anyone that believes the setbacks in their life are too much to overcome. Demetrius has made it his mission to help people see that there is hope in all areas of their life, and by changing just a few things, they can achieve the life they have always desired.

Demetrius is a Man of God, exceptional father of two girls and four boys, and "Paw-Paw" to six growing grandchildren. He is a solid example of what it means to live through life's stressors and own up to your failures. He desires to be globally known for his ability and great passion for faith, family, entrepreneurship and business.

CHAPTER 16

THE ART OF LIVING

BY DIANE THOMAS GALLOWAY

At an age of discovery and in the age of Aquarius we are here to continue the journey of life as we know it. However, at the young age of 17 years old, I got pregnant and felt the wrath of discouragement, and desperation started to be the norm. I had just finished high school and I had taken my "O" Levels from England which was the exam we take (from the University of Oxford) as our final exam, and I got a degree in Spanish and Latin. My parents were so upset because they had such high expectations for me that my pregnancy changed all our lives.

You see, as I found out that I was pregnant, my father was about to kill me. So, I decided to commit suicide, and then I met a beautiful person who was an accountant. He encouraged me to 'keep the faith' and not to lose hope, and that my father was not going to kill me and that he was going to stick with me through it all. Let us recollect, when I found out that I was pregnant, I had to send my father a letter to tell him, and at the same time, to ask his forgiveness. My father and I were very close. I was his first born and 'the apple of his eye' so the disappointment was great for both my parents.

My father moved to the U.S. Virgin Islands because employment was almost non-existent in my island home of Trinidad, and my mother then followed. We had nannies, and when the news was received, they headed back home. At first, my mother and I felt like crawling under a rock. Then my father came home. I was shivering in my shoes when my father arrived. It was the day before Carnival, and being from Trinidad, it was held the same time as Carnival in Brazil – every year it's a few days before Lent. On the Tuesday morning, I had breakfast and told my mother that my stomach was griping. She told me to drink some orange peel tea. I did and it got worse when I told her she was here to enjoy the Carnival with my husband and me, and that I was responsible for my troubles and I should bear them alone.

I was in labor for eight hours until a neighbour came by to check on my sister, and I told him how I felt. He called his sister, who told her mother who told me to get ready for the hospital. My handsome son was born in February, on Ash Wednesday morning at 2 a.m.

I was delighted and scared at the same time. Neither of my parents were at the hospital and my siblings were too young to come, so I had my baby alone and I took him home alone in a taxi. You see, when I was about to tell my boyfriend at the time about the baby, there was another there when I went to his home, so I cried my heart out and left never telling him. He found out months later from my best friend at the time.

Now that my baby was here, I had to feed and clothe him. So, my father went back to St. Croix and after having searched 'my eyeballs out' for work in Trinidad, I had to write a letter to my father asking his forgiveness and asking him to send for me to come to the Virgin Islands to find work to support myself and my baby. He agreed and filed the papers, and I was the first to join him. I looked for employment taking the bus and walking most of the time in the hot sun until my complexion was pitch black. I then saw an advertisement in the paper for a waitress, and told my father that I was going to take it. He said, "No daughter of mine is going to be a waitress because of the stigma attached to the job." I had to agree and so I kept looking until I found one at the Timex Corporation and started assembling watches. It was there I met an interesting person, but that's another topic. I was not challenged there and after six months, I started looking for something better. I found employment at the Bank of America and became a loan clerk. I stayed for a year. However, before that, as I was walking to get the taxi home, I met my first husband who was a talker and a jovial, funny person who always had to be the center of attention. We dated for six months. My father did not like him, but my mother accepted him with open arms because she felt that since I had a child, I was lucky that someone wanted me, and was pushing for the marriage just as much as my then husband. But my father did not like the idea, in fact, he almost did not attend the wedding. Lesson number one – when your parent or parents dislike your significant other, it's a sign to think twice. They see something you do not. A word to the wise. . .

Needless to say, I got married and we rented a house because he was one of the best carpenters and made good money. I got pregnant again and was having my second son and we named him Kerry. My husband was another handsome king, and I thought I was very happy. His family were Seventh Day Adventists, so I joined the church and there is where I began the journey of health. We then moved to Florida where he got a job with the union, and the pay was great. I did not have to work, so I stayed at home with the kids. My first was four years old and the second was two. Then I got pregnant again with my daughter. Beautiful. . . my first and only girl. I was in seventh heaven.

We all know that everything has seasons. You see, in between times, my husband at the time had a great job. Word started spreading about his fine carpentry, and as he became even more popular, he started working late at women's houses. Some were single, some were married, and the temptation was too much, and he got caught up. I was insulted more and more – morning, noon and night! Before he entered the door, he would say. "I bet the food tastes horrible," or, "I do not like the smell." And then he would sit down to eat and say, "Honey, what a wonderful meal!" So, he was a Jeckle and Hyde.

One day, his sister started saying things about my son to her sister-in-law – that he did not know who his father was, and the word got back to me. I was advised to tell my son that my husband was not his father before he heard it from the wrong people, or in the wrong way. So, I decided to have a talk with my son and spoke to my husband first, and was told that it was not his business and that I could do whatever I wanted. So, I decided to take my son out and talk to him. My son said he knew he was not his father by the feeling. Then, he immediately said he wanted to see his father.

I made the contacts and it was arranged. My husband and the kids were to go to Trinidad for a vacation because he was from another country and never went there. However, after all the arrangements were made, my husband said he changed his mind and was not going, and that I was not to take any of the other children that were his with me. I then called my sister and asked her to stay with the others, because I was going. You see, by this time, I was tired of the mental abuse of being told when to get up, when to sit down, and how stupid I was to think, and that every idea I had never made sense, and that nothing I tried could ever work because I only had stupid ideas. Now, I was church secretary, youth leader, missionary outreach leader and on the church Board. By now, if you do not know that your mate, husband, wife or significant other can be so jealous of you that they make a concerted effort to sabotage you and your entire life, you're wrong! I was cussed out Monday to Monday, and mentally abused from the time he walked into the house to the time he left the next morning.

Our sex was always on his terms. If I said "no" my clothes were dragged off me and I had to submit in order to get a night's rest. Today, it would be called rape, but back then the church called it 'be in submission to your husband.' When I talked to my pastor about it, it was as if they were saying that some women do not get any, and you should be glad that it's every night. Well, to say the least, after we went to Trinidad and came back, I got such a beating because my husband thought I was disobedient and needed to be reprimanded, so I was asked, "What happened?" When I said nothing, I was punched so hard that I fell to the ground with my nose bleeding and my daughter screaming.

Because my sister took the boys to the store, I was kicked and dragged to the kitchen to prepare his meals, since I was not to be a wife and just prepare his meals. With my nose spewing blood, and my daughter just eight years old and screaming, he had a pot and was holding me at the stove to cook. The phone rang when my sister came back, she saw me crying and bleeding, and it was my father on the phone. He gave me the phone and my father said "Ann," as he called me, "What's wrong?" and I said, "Nothing, Daddy." He hung up, called his three sisters who lived in N.Y. with him and asked them to call, because something was wrong with his daughter.

I have an aunt who was known for her words that she uttered with great description. I was on the phone next and he says, "Auntie." I could not repeat what she said to him, it would have to be edited out. I called the police the day after and they said the only choice was to have him arrested. Many of us women make the mistake because it's our children's fathers and say "No," then we are stuck with a recurring situation. We then went through a 'rough and tumble' time, and later, when I had enough, I decided to leave.

One day he asked my second son to go to work with him. All he talked about to him was me being unfaithful (to our twelve-year-old). My son responded, "My mother will never do that." He then hit him with his fist in his temple. My son ran into the house screaming, and when he told me what had happened, I immediately 'lost it' and all the anger of being beaten came back to me. I was previously given a butcher knife as a gift for watching a vacuum cleaner demo and it was in my kitchen cabinet. I jumped on the counter, scaled it like a monkey, got the knife and held it to his navel, and told him that I would twist it if he ever touched me or abused any of my children. He trembled like a leaf and begged my brother to come and get me because I was going crazy.

It is something in life that you do not ever want to get to, where you have to hurt someone to save yourself or your children's life. I sympathize with the women in prison who have had to make those terrible decisions that cost them their freedom. So, as you contemplate a relationship, marriage, or just dating, choose wisely. Think about it. Get to know the person; remember, internet dating is dangerous and risky. Listen to your parents or elders. Seek their advice. This will save you a lot of heartache later. I wish I had.

Although I had three beautiful kids, one, my second – Kerry, was killed by a drunk driver. All the love I could ever imagine that a son could give to his mother, he gave to me. And for that, I will forever be grateful, and I dedicate this article to him, as well as all my children and grandchildren.

I then got married for a second time to an artist. He was a man I knew for five years. We had lots of fun, but after we got married I found out how controlling he was, and I ran from him after three months, because in my mind, I saw the picture of my first husband forming, and so I ran for cover. Well, there was a third time, and I fell in love with a Mexican man. He was kind and loving, and if my feet hurt, he would rub them and cry with me if I was in any pain. He helped me with my business and I got breakfast in bed and dinner too, and you might ask what went wrong? The problem was that he drank . . . only a little, I thought.

After we got married, I found out he was a real alcoholic. I tried with him, but it was unbearable after eleven years. His family is wonderful. You will find that not all of your husband's family will like you, nor will you like all of them, but we were happy, I thought. That lasted until I had to go back and forth because of my business, and he got involved with someone else and everything went south. Mexico is a beautiful place, the people are beautiful and like in every country, there are good, bad, and indifferent. In general, people are people. I will not say I would not get married again, but this time I will make better choices.

I will look before I leap. And for the women who might read this, do not settle nor take abuse of any kind, whether verbal or physical. You can agree and not lose your self-esteem. Never stop trying to improve yourself. I am now the CEO of the Herbal Gardens, a company started in 1985 after I left my husband. I owned five stores and a restaurant. I closed them all except one after my son got killed, but with determination and the will to never give up, I am still learning and growing. I looked in my library and found a course I ordered years ago from Nightingale Conant, and a book called *Thought Vibration*. I am so honored to be given this opportunity to even share a chapter or a verse in this book that my heart is overwhelmed. You see, dreams do come true once you dream big enough.

You see, I could have quit and gone on welfare when my son was born, or just settled for someone else to be responsible for him. I was told to put him up for adoption because I was so young. However, I chose not to, because it was my responsibility to take care of whatever mess I created, and to make a difference.

When I started my business, I had no money, two boxes of herbs, and a desire to win. I joined a 'susu' as we called it. That's where groups of people pool their money together every week, and every week it's someone else's turn to use it. That is how I started – with just enough for the first and last month's rent. My landlord wanted to know when my goods were coming to open the store, and I said, "Very soon."

Man's will to push forward is the key to life's journey, and the art of living. May you be blessed beyond measure in the pursuit of your dreams.

About Diane

Diane Thomas Galloway was born on the island of Trinidad and lived there until the age of 18. She then migrated to St. Croix, U.S.V.I. and later to Florida. Miss Galloway is the first of seven children. Her parents were Lloyd and Annetta Thomas who were married for 43 years until her father died of lung cancer at the young age of 67. Her mother lived to the ripe old age of 94. Miss Galloway graduated from High School with a degree in Spanish and Latin from the University of Oxford, England. Her career spans over decades – from the learning years at the Timex Cooperation to the banking industry as a Teller Loan Clerk and a proof operator working for Bank of America and First National City Bank of New York. Later, she joined another financial institution, American Express, and had the position of Customer Service Rep. and resigned as a Fraud Analyst.

Diane then made the decision to enter the world of business on a different level by taking on the task of being her own boss. Miss Galloway has her own business called The Herbal Gardens, which is a Herbal Health Food Store with a great difference, because they manufacture their own line of products which are sold internationally. This is a family-operated business that has evolved over some three decades plus.

She is the proud to have given birth to three wonderful children, two boys and a girl, one of whom, Kerry Michael Galloway, was unfortunately killed by a drunk, and to whom she dedicates all to his memory. Jessel was her first born and Adeline the last. Miss Galloway also is the proud grandparent of Zaakira, Johann, Kerry and Cassie.

She has served her community for decades and is a member of the Lauderhill Chamber of Commerce and the Ft. Lauderdale Chamber. She has done radio for over 30 years and a monthly T.V. show in Trinidad. She has been featured on local Channel 7 news, in the *Sun Sentinel* newspaper, and the *Miami Herald*.

Miss Galloway, as a Herbalist, has been helping and serving the community for several years and has no plans at this time to retire. Her hobbies are reading, dancing, writing and travel. She is thankful and grateful for being a member of Global Information Network.

Contact information:
- www.theherbalgardens.com
- 954-584-6601 or 1-877-626-4112

CHAPTER 17

LIFE BEYOND THE SCAR
THE POWER OF NEVER
GIVING UP

BY DANIELLE GORDON

Maybe the journey isn't so much about becoming anything.
Maybe it's about un-becoming everything that isn't really you,
so you can be who you were meant to be in the first place.
~ Author Unknown

The analogy between myself and a war veteran: When a veteran comes back and has seen more than they ever wanted to see, or thought when going to war that they could handle it. But coming back home, they just are not the same anymore. People don't see it. It's not visible. This is wearing on one's thoughts that can control the mind. . . feeling so misunderstood. It's so easy when feeling like this to put up a wall to protect yourself. Even though it would make a world of difference for someone to see the unbalance or the aloofness within the one living with PTSD, to take five minutes to just ask if the person is ok, allowing for time to connect with them. Ask them if there is anything you can do to help? If you see someone struggling, do you just judge them and walk away or do you give them five minutes of your time?

Has there been a point in your life that you have had a hard time getting over. It just became a part of you and you had such a hard time shaking it? This is my story of a breakthrough transformation. How I went from a victim to owning my power as a survivor and making my dreams my reality.

On a train heading west from Winnipeg, Manitoba for what I thought my mom and I were going to see family in Revelstoke, BC. She then told me that she had left my step-dad and in fact we were moving. My heart broke. I was so super close to my step-dad. I never got a proper good-bye.

Life turned on me as I once knew it, at the age of 11. Caught at the wrong place at the wrong time. I was viciously assaulted. I was thrown around like a dog grabbing onto a toy or prey and shaking the s*** out of it. I was on my knees, and fighting for my life, I looked up and just begged him to stop. I felt so overpowered and defeated. Eventually, when I was let go, with evidence on me, I ran (what seemed like across town) to where my mom was. She had instantly seen me, and addressed her concern of what happened. Later that evening she confronted my abuser with four of us there. She after brought me to a room, told me she knew it was true, but I was never allowed to tell anyone. She silenced me!! Too young and naive to take the right responsibility upon myself to go to the police, not knowing how the impact would affect me for years to come.

My life spiralled out of control between the ages of 11-13 when my mom finally sent me to live with my biological dad. I had never lived without my mom. I had spent lots of time with my grandparents on the farm in Manitoba or spent lots of time with my aunts, uncles, and cousins, but never lived away from my mom. I was getting involved with the wrong kids with the same emotional attention seeking outcry as I had myself. Sex, drugs, and partying... I started out running away just for the thrill of it. I was thirteen, living in a major city where running the streets didn't sound as scary to me then as it does now. It was just too much for my dad. He didn't know what he was in for, I guess you can say it was a relationship gone south before it even began. If he would have only known, he could have probably been more prepared and even understood what he was getting himself into and why. I missed my mom so she made the move to live with my dad and I until we got our own place.

Eventually, my mom got me out of Vancouver and made the move to Whitehorse, Yukon. It was just yet another new place to carry on my precarious behaviour. Needless to say, I had just failed Grade 8, so I was now restarting Grade 8. Not only was I in a new school with new kids, in a new town, but I was repeating Grade 8 with younger kids. My pride was hurt!! My mom was a hairdresser by day and a bartender by night.

That's when she met her husband. I would wake up morning after morning, look into her bedroom to see if she was sleeping in her bed but she just wasn't there anymore.

Meanwhile, a girlfriend and I kept on hanging out with these much older guys. She and I were in the same class one day and exchanged a very personal note that should have never been shared between us in class. The teacher caught us and in front of a very packed class, began to read it out loud. We both bolted out the classroom door and right out of the school. I never did look back. With my mom not at home anymore, I was on the run.

I was a little lost soul trying to find my way. Between Whitehorse, Vancouver, and Winnipeg, I was on and off the streets. . . staying with anyone who would take me in. I never really stayed anywhere long enough, until I was on the go again. At times, I would walk around aimlessly at all hours of the night or feeling so desperate I would hitch hike in hopes of being given a place to sleep.

I became pregnant at the age of sixteen with a baby boy that I just could not keep. I was too young to know how to look after him when I couldn't even look after myself. Wandering aimlessly in extreme winter weather in Winnipeg, I landed him in the hospital fighting for his life. Eventually, my biological dad and his wife stepped in and took over custody, taking him away from me. As hard as that was, and at what seemed so heartbreaking at that time, it was the very best thing that could have happened to my son.

At the age of twenty-three, I had my second son. Not wanting to lose a second child, I continued to battle my demons, and through it all I fought to become a better person. I never wanted Sheldon to walk a mile in my shoes and eventually moved to Kelowna, BC from the Yukon for a better life for him and myself. Sheldon was three.

I met my amazing husband in May of 2000. Together with his fifteen-year-old daughter, we became a blended family. I continued to go through growing pains and the lessons of life, with a victim's state of mind, but he gave me stability, support, acceptance, grounded me, loved me, and encouraged me.

In March of 2011, I won VIP tickets to see Dr. Wayne Dyer. With tears streaming down my face, I listened to him share his story. Dr. Dyer and I had a very personal one-on-one conversation where in that moment I knew I had to go from victim to survivor and take a stance in my truth. That April, coming from such a place of peace and forgiveness in my heart, I emailed my abuser, ready to move beyond what had happened to me. It backfired on me. My mom turned against me for protecting him. His mom was emailing me threatening emails. The betrayal of my mom knowing the truth and telling our family that I was lying took me down hard. I was ousted and since then time and time again, I watch family gatherings and weddings that I'm just not invited to anymore.

With mass grief, betrayal, and a broken heart, I have seen my darkest days, cried my deepest core tears, and screamed at God and the Universe to either take me or change the path I was on. I was done with the broken heart and I was done with the struggle!!

You don't know how strong you are until being strong
is the only choice you have.
~ Bob Marley

Your journey has molded you for the greater good. It was
exactly what needed to be. Don't think you've lost time.
It took each and every situation you have.
~ Asha Tyson

Soon after that is when I learnt and began my journey training in a Law of Attraction Life Coaching course and Ruben West's Black Belt Speaker training.

I reflect on my public speaking and sharing my story publicly after being silenced for twenty-seven years. After I did speak out, I lost the core of my extensively large family. How scary that was or is, but I know people need my courage. People need my voice. There are so many people out there that hide within themselves, hiding behind the silence because of fearing judgement or of breaking the family silence code. So, they see the impossible and get caught in a rut that does nothing but self-sabotage. I know, I lived like that for too many years. Partying day after day, year after year for years, staying numb.

To know that as hard and as scary as it was for me to break my silence, and fearing the judgements of my family, taking that stance and breaking my silence anyways has been the most terrifying but freeing gift that I could have ever done for myself. This was a case of taking my power back, really learning what my power felt like, honouring who I am and who I was meant to be.

The Power of our beliefs can work in either direction
to become life affirming or life denying.
~ Greg Braden

STRATEGIES FOR THE MINDSET SHIFT

#1. ~ Shift from victim to survivor.
The world is your oyster. Everything in life is up to you – every choice, every decision, every action, how you approach things. It is all up to you. Do what you have to do with action RIGHT NOW!! Start by loving yourself first. Connect and resonate with how that truly feels. Use that feeling mind-tool to always refer back to exactly how that feels. You have everything you need inside of you.

This is up to you!!

#2. ~ Set your mind on what you want and be clear.
It doesn't matter who you are or how old you are. You can be a high school dropout, homeless and living in shelters or on the streets, you can be beyond 60, 70 or 80. . . it is never too late to go after whatever you want. Never sell yourself short on limited beliefs. See your vision and know your why. Be completely unstoppable.

I heard Doreen Virtue say this and loved it: *When you ask the universe what it is you want, order it like you would order off a menu to a waitress/waiter in a restaurant.*

#3. ~ Watch your words and thoughts that you put out there to the Universe.
People get so stuck in their beliefs and what you think you become. That's a key factor in why people struggle. They get so wrapped up in their negative or overwhelming thoughts and they don't know which way to turn. What to do next.

My example... This opportunity of being an author in this book. I kept saying to the universe: "Universe, please show me where the next opportunity for my success is." I knew I had wanted to be in this book as I had looked into the opportunity previously. I would carry Brian Tracy's book, *Goals,* almost everywhere with me. It was never too far behind me. Keep your eye on the prize! Never come from a place of need when putting your manifesting thoughts out there.

A common struggle is that people will focus on what's wrong instead of focusing on what's right. *Why worry about what hasn't happened yet?*

#4. ~ Be so driven that you will do whatever it takes for however long it takes until you are living that dream you were once dreaming about.

My example... In Jan./Feb. 2017, my husband and I toured the mainland of Mexico which was seven weeks of ocean-front holiday. We love the ocean. My heart and soul connect to being by the water. We were two weeks into what was already an amazing trip. In Barra de Navidad, we had a beautiful room with a big balcony in which we were so close that it felt like we were on top of the water. We would go on a nightly moonlight walk down the melancon. I fell completely in love with it all. There is nothing like the feeling when you realize you are living the dream you once only thought about. Now my mantra is: I'm going to celebrate my dreams and when I achieve those dreams, I will dream bigger dreams.

#5. ~ Be thankful and be appreciative about everything.
I say 'thank you' to almost everything by habit and I love hearing it from other people.

My example... the epiphany that I was connecting to in Barra of completely being in awe of such deep appreciation and gratefulness of really how far I had come and that I was living my life I could only dream of.

~Gratitude turns what we have into enough, and more. It turns denial into acceptance, chaos into order, confusion into clarity... it makes sense of our past, brings peace for today, and creates a vision for tomorrow. ~ Melody Beattie

#6. ~ <u>Visualize clearly the partner you want to fall in love with.</u> What is it you are looking for? You want a partner that plays sports. If it's golf and you don't know how to play, learn. Baseball, get into playing ball. If you want a quiet guy, start hanging out at the library. Whatever it is that you are seeking in a partner. Go there!!

What is it that drives your passion? What is your absolute favourite thing to do?

CLOSING THOUGHTS

Dream life so big that the universe has no choice but to continually give to you in a flow of abundance. Start your day before you get out of bed, and go to sleep at night connecting to what that feels like to be so thankful and appreciative for everything. It's the way you perceive life that defines how you live your life.

Always know, and in those times of chaos keep saying it will all work out. Allow it to happen the way it is supposed to happen. Set yourself free from the ones that have hurt you, scarred you. Love yourself and the life you live so much that it naturally connects you to forgiving. You have everything in you to start making your dreams your reality RIGHT NOW!!

Wishes for all the abundance that is so rightfully yours.
Believe and trust. My love to all of you.
~ Danielle Gordon

About Danielle

Danielle Gordon is an Entrepreneur, Law of Attraction Life Coach, Speaker, and Author.

She has a very powerful, transformational, breakthrough story that started at the age of eleven when she faced a very vicious assault - which resulted in living with PTSD - and landed her on and off the streets as a runaway homeless teen for most of her teen years. She faced the adversities of shame and betrayal. After keeping that secret within her for 27 years, she spoke out by confronting her abuser, only for it to backfire on her, and she was ousted by her extensively large family. She then faced her darkest days, cried her deepest core tears through mass grief with what felt like re-victimization. Suicide became an option when she was done with the broken heart and the struggle. Her driven determination and the mindset of never giving up got her through living her life as that runaway teen, and allowed her to move on to live a life she once could only dream about.

Her empathy and driven passion is about bringing the very best out in people in both their personal and business lives. In her Life Coaching sessions, she guides you through visual meditations, raising your vibration to a higher frequency within you, shifting your thoughts and connecting you with the Law of Attraction thought tools – which manifest game-changing shifts that create results. Bringing herself through her own coaching practices have resulted in from her being able to sell her mother-in-law's house to the opportunities that come with being in this book, *Driven*. She's a natural at manifesting.

She is driven to continually thrive by living the very best version of herself, bringing her authentic self to her audience and clientele. She is an opportunist utilizing opportunities with driven motivation and determination.

Danielle was born into an extensively large Metis family on June 15th, 1972 in Winnipeg, Manitoba, Canada. She is currently married to her 'bestest' friend whom she met in May of 2000, and married him in Sept. 2012. She's a mom, step-mom, and loves being a young grandma. Her little blended family is where her heart belongs.

For Danielle, inspired by her travel with her mom and her mom's husband,

and experiencing many foreign lands, she would rather have had nothing and all the love in the world from her mom and mom's husband than have everything and not feel loved. She continues the love of travel with her husband. They both ride Harley Davidsons and make their home as Canadian Snowbirds in Arizona for six months in the winter. Their home in Canada is Canada's destination spot in the summer, the sunny Okanagan. Danielle loves travelling where she always seems to be on some amazing and fun-filled adventure.

She is also co-authoring two other books, *Leaving Our Legacy* with Women on a Mission Enterprises and *The Time is Now* with Ruben West, by whom she has been professionally trained as a Public Speaker.

CHAPTER 18

DRIVEN TO BE SUCCESSFUL IN BUSINESS

BY SCOTT BURNETT, ESQ.

When I started my own business, it was a dream come true. Finally, I thought, I do not have to work for anyone else ever again. I am free! I can work when I want and all my successes would be my own.

I didn't know a lot about running a business when I started. In hindsight, I can see that I didn't have any idea what I was doing. I did not have any systems in place. I had no discipline to my day. I didn't know anything about taxes, and/or my responsibilities regarding them. I was just spending my days putting out fires, and making phone calls. I figured if I work hard, then everything else would just take care of itself.

After a few years, I received a letter in the mail that would change my life. It was a letter from the IRS. I was about to be audited. Nothing to worry about, right? I filed my tax returns every year. I didn't cheat. I had professional assistance. I hired a CPA for my company that was highly recommended. Further, I met with him every year. He never seemed concerned about any of my deductions or my numbers. I thought, OK, I am going to be fine.

The audit lasted several days. At the end of the day, I owed the IRS over sixty-thousand dollars ($60,000.00) in taxes and penalties. Ouch!

I called that $60,000 tax liability my tuition payment in the School of Hard Knocks! That audit changed my career. I realized that day that running a business is more than just making money and working hard. A business owner must know more about business responsibilities. He or she needs to know more about taxes.

I wondered how many other people were out there just like me – hard workers, but lacking fundamental business training. I became obsessed with all things business and taxes. I would never be a victim again!

Below are some great tips that I learned from my early career and audit. I have implemented these things over the years and I found they made a huge difference for me:

I. RUNNING A BUSINESS IS HARD WORK! PERIOD

In our society, I think we shy away from telling people tough things. We don't want to make people feel uncomfortable. This is especially true in business. But people want to know the truth. So here it is: Running a successful business is hard work.

It just is. Don't be duped into believing anything else. It is a hard hustle. And let's face it, not everyone can handle it. If it was easy, then everybody would do it.

The truth is that running a business requires effort. But that doesn't mean it must be hard. It's how you view what you are doing that makes all the difference.

II. TURN HARD "WORK" INTO PASSION

Since running a business will be tough, you need to love what you do! I mean this sincerely, if you don't love what you're doing you will have a tough time being successful in your business. Your passion for what you do becomes your fuel. You will face obstacles and challenges in your business and it will be your passion for what you do that will nourish and sustain you.

If you love what you do, then the hard work becomes easier. There is a passion to grow. A passion to learn. A passion to succeed. Loving what you do makes life and work easier. It's not a job. It's your passion.

Success in business begins and ends with your mind set. You have a real choice here. You can work hard and grind out every day. Or you can work hard, but enjoy it because you love what you're doing.

III. SELF EVALUATION: WOULD I HIRE ME?

If you're reading this, you are probably already running a business on your own. So, of course, you would hire you! That's a stupid question, right?

But would you want someone to work like you do?

The number one thing I learned after I started my business was that I stopped working regular hours. I had the freedom to come late or leave early from work whenever I wanted. I probably took off more time than I should. Of course, I justified it by saying that I was the boss and I could do what I wanted.

But I realized if I had an employee who worked like I did, I would fire them!

- "What do you mean you want to leave early?"
- "What do you mean you will get to it later?"
- "What do you mean you want another day off?"

Just because I had the freedom to do whatever I wanted didn't mean I should. I needed to check in at work. I needed to be a better employee for my company.

This is probably the biggest mistake I see other business owners make. They simply are not disciplined about their time.

IV. SCHEDULING YOUR TIME AT WORK

We are always busy at work. But would you rather be busy, or productive? Being productive requires discipline. We need to look at time as a commodity. If you don't have a schedule to your day, it is very easy to spend a day being busy putting out fires, but not producing anything tangible at the end of the day.

How do you stop being busy and start being productive? Schedule your work days!

Because our time is flexible, we tend to start and end projects at different times throughout the week. We basically do whatever we want. No structure or schedule. We just keep ourselves busy throughout the day.

What a schedule will provide you is more of a rhythm to your day, and it will give you more focused energy when it's needed most. For example, if your business has prospecting calls to be made, then the best time to do that is in the morning. That is when you are fresh and have lots of energy. Further, it gives people an opportunity to call you back if you missed them when you called earlier.

Below is my sample work day schedule:

Scott Burnett Work Schedule

5:00 AM to 6:00 AM	Wake up / Coffee / Read
6:00 AM to 7:00 AM	Get in the Gym / Workout
7:00 AM to 8:00 AM	Shower / Dressed / Breakfast / Commute
8:00 AM to 8:30 AM	Check Phone Messages, Emails, Write Things to do
8:30 AM to 12:00 PM	Phone Calls / Clients / Prospecting
12:00 PM to 1:30 PM	Lunch / Personal Time
1:30 PM to 3:30 PM	Return Calls / Email Response
3:30 PM to 4:30 PM	Projects / Learning
4:30 PM to 5:00 PM	Banking / Pay Bills

That's it! Every day the same formula. Now, if you are looking at that and it seems robotic to you, I understand. I thought so too when I first started. But what I discovered was that I was more productive. I did more than just come in everyday and start doing something. It's more disciplined than just being busy. Its real production. It became my job description!

Now I find that I have more free time. More time for my family and friends. More time to enjoy other things than I ever did before. Who knew! It's amazing what a little scheduling can do.

Now, this is my final product. But it took me a while to figure out what worked best for me.

For example, I used to do my banking first thing in the morning. That didn't work out because I would stress about bills and it affected my energy during the day. So, I moved it to the end of the day. Second, I used to only take an hour for lunch. I learned that I needed more time to re-charge. My schedule required several revisions before it became my routine.

V. HOW DO YOU START YOUR OWN WORK SCHEDULE?

Start out with a rough outline of your day. Then look at what you do and when you do it. Make sure you write things down that you must get done. Make sure the important things are done first in your scheduling!

Once you have a rough outline written out, start following it. Give it a couple of weeks. Does it work for you? Next, if necessary, start refining it. You may find, like I did, that some things work better at different times of the day for you. Don't be a slave to the schedule. Be flexible, but be disciplined.

Test it for yourself. I am confident that you will become more focused in your business and more productive.

The trouble with free enterprise is that it doesn't mean free time! The old saying: Time is money, applies perfectly here. Every minute, hour, day, week or month needs to produce results.

Make your time work for you!

VI. YOUR CPA IS NOT RESPONSIBLE FOR YOUR TAXES -YOU ARE!

"My CPA takes care of my taxes!"

I thought that. Until I got the tax bill from my audit. I believed that if I was doing something wrong with my taxes, my CPA would see it and tell me. If there was something better I should do, he would tell me. But that just isn't the dynamic between the tax payer and the tax preparer.

Examine the relationship between you and your tax professional. You write all the checks and make all the payments in your business during the year. When you meet with your tax professional, it is usually <u>after</u> the year is over. You meet, give them all the information, and they prepare your tax return. But they are not conducting a tax class for you. They're not in that meeting to teach you tax rules.

Your tax professional isn't determining what is deductible for you because that decision was made by you the moment you spent the money. Their job is to put your expenses in the right box on your tax return. But whether that expense was deductible or not was already determined by you the moment you made the purchase. If that expense required more documentation (tax diary) or was only partially deductible, that needed to be known by you.

But it is even worse. A recent government survey determined that the average business owner in America overpays their taxes by a whopping $11,000 plus a year. That means not only are the deductions you are claiming a potential problem, but you're not claiming enough of them!

In business, tax knowledge is critical. Whenever you overpay your taxes you lose profit. Now, you don't need to become a tax expert, but you do need to understand three important things. This is all you need to know to be more successful in reducing your business and personal taxes.

1. MASTER <u>FIVE</u> BASIC DEDUCTIONS:
Some deductions only require proof of purchase – for example, purchases of equipment or marketing. However, some expenses require what the IRS calls

substantiation. There are five deductions that require more than a receipt. They are:

- Entertainment
- Travel
- Gifting
- Vehicle
- Home Office

This is the most fertile ground for an auditor. Most business owners do not know that they need to keep a tax diary on these expenses to protect these deductions. The good news, you don't need to learn the whole tax code. But you must master these five.

2. YOUR BUSINESS MODEL DETERMINES YOUR PERSONAL TAXES: The way you run your business: sole proprietor, corporation, or LLC will determine how much personal tax you pay. Each business model is unique in the way it can pay its owner. This is because the IRS regulates the way an owner can take money out of their company. Knowing this could save you thousands of dollars every year.

3. TAX PREPARATION IS NOT TAX PLANNING: The biggest problem between the business owner and their tax professional is that we expect too much from a once a year meeting. Usually, we meet our CPA once a year, and then they prepare a tax return for us. But if you are serious about reducing taxes you need to meet your tax professional before the year is over. That is tax planning. Talk and meet to discuss opportunities and challenges. Ask questions. You might be surprised at how many opportunities there are for you to modify your expenses and reduce taxes.

VII. CONCLUSION

Business success can be dependable and predictable. Successful business owners are passionate, disciplined and have a basic understanding about their taxes. It's your money, so always remember – the more you know, the less you will owe.

About Scott

Scott Burnett is a business coach and a nationally-recognized speaker and author who has been teaching and sharing business and tax tips with audiences all over the country for over ten years. Scott is one of the nation's leading legal authorities on asset protection and taxes for business owners in North America. His diverse legal background includes being a Deputy District Attorney for Santa Barbara County, California, and five years as a trial attorney in his own private practice. He has taught thousands and thousands of people how to reduce taxes and protect their assets.

Scott's passion is teaching. He loves to share business and tax tips with business owners to help them achieve greater financial success. His ability to explain complicated material in an uncomplicated and entertaining manner has made him a highly sought-after trainer and speaker throughout the country.

Scott is the CEO of Burnett and Associates, Inc., a corporation providing business and tax education to business owners across North America. He is an approved CPE provider for the National Association of State Boards of Accountancy. He is also on the Executive Board for the Association of Network Marketing Professionals, and sits on the Boards of Directors for over 200 separate businesses. He was also selected as one of America's PremierExperts® and has been quoted in *Newsweek, The Wall Street Journal, USA Today* and *Inc. Magazine* as well as featured on MSN, CNN, and Fox News television speaking on business regulations and taxes. Scott was recently accepted as a Council Member for the Global Entrepreneurship Initiative, and will be a featured presenter at The FORUM™ held at the United Nations.

Scott recognizes that the legal and tax systems do not do enough to educate business owners. Today's entrepreneurs lack basic business and tax knowledge, and do not know where to go to get it. Thus, they will always be victims in a system that preys on their lack of knowledge. Scott is committed to helping his clients master the fundamentals of proper business operations, and helping each one achieve greater profitability.

You can connect with Scott at:
- Scott@BurnettandAssociates.com
- www.facebook.com/burnettassociates